IRISH INDUSTRY:
STRUCTURE AND PERFORMANCE

IRISH INDUSTRY:
STRUCTURE AND PERFORMANCE

PATRICK O'MALLEY

GILL AND MACMILLAN
Dublin

BARNES AND NOBLE, PUBLISHERS
New York

First published in Ireland 1971 by
GILL AND MACMILLAN LTD
2 Belvedere Place
Dublin 1

in London through association with the
MACMILLAN
Group of Publishing Companies

First published in the United States of America, 1972 by
BARNES & NOBLE, PUBLISHERS
New York, New York

Gill & Macmillan SBN: 7171 0526 1
Barnes & Noble ISBN: 389 04453 9

Jacket design by Des Fitzgerald

Printing History
10 9 8 7 6 5 4 3 2 1

Printed and bound in the Republic of Ireland by the Book Printing Division of
Smurfit Print and Packaging Limited, Dublin

TO MY MOTHER

ACKNOWLEDGEMENTS

THE author wishes to thank Professor James Meenan and Dr E. A. Attwood, who directed the thesis on which this book is based; the Director of An Foras Talúntais for facilities; Mr J. Connolly, Statistics Department, Miss H. O'Donnell and Miss E. Flynn, and the technical staff in the Rural Economy Division of An Foras Talúntais for assistance in the many tedious calculations which were necessary; Miss Anne-Marie Boyle and Miss Kathy Derimer for typing the script; and the late Mrs Mary Loughlin for her constant encouragement. The author would also like to thank Dr Brendan Walsh, Economic and Social Research Institute, for his invaluable assistance and advice in the course of preparing this book for publication.

Particular acknowledgement is due to Professor P. S. Florence whose pioneering work *Investment Location and Size of Plant* is the source work, especially for methodology for the first three chapters; to Dr W. E. G. Salter whose empirical study of inter-industry productivity movements in the U.K. in Part II of *Productivity and Technical Change* is the basis for much of the analysis in Chapter 5; and to Dr John Cornwall, formerly Professor of Economics at Tufts University, Medford, Mass., and currently Professor of Economics at the University of Southern Illinois, for the concept of economic growth as a process of transformation.

Tufts University
Medford, Mass.

Note: Numbers in brackets through the text are references to the bibliography given at the end of the book.

CONTENTS

1 THE LOCATION OF INDUSTRIAL ACTIVITY

1.1 Introduction

One of the many problems facing developing countries is the imbalance of industrial activity a problem which, in Ireland, has caused a great deal of concern but which is still far from solution. Since such an imbalance may be detrimental to the over-all development of a society, and may lead to waste in its use of human and social overhead resources, an investigation of its causes provides, perhaps, the best starting point for this book.

The process of industrialisation involves not only the creation of new industry but also its introduction to specific regions; this raises the question whether the existing location pattern of industry is the result of haphazard and fortuitous circumstances or whether some set of factors exists which accounts for it.

In the latter case knowledge of these factors may be put to several uses. First, specific industries may be identified which could individually, and in groups, operate efficiently in different regions. It is important to do so at present since to a large extent the promotion of industrial growth and the diversification of industry are undertaken by such official agencies as the Industrial Development Authority and the Industrial Credit Company. Indeed, some newly-established enterprises have failed because they were set up on social rather than economic grounds. Second, by clarifying the nature of an industry's location structure it is easier to estimate its growth rate and the total contribution it will make towards the development of a region since both will depend to a considerable extent on whether the industry is an induced or autonomous activity (see page 14). Finally, since sustained economic growth requires a highly-integrated economic structure it is necessary to know what inter-relationships exist between specific industries and the degree and nature of their dependence.

1

Four main exercises are, therefore, carried out in this chapter: (i) computation of some measures to summarise the location structure of an industry; (ii) application of these measures to Irish industries; (iii) examination of the results in order to establish the factors responsible for the observed trends; and (iv) delineation of the locational inter-relationships between specific industries.

1.2 The measurement of an industry's location structure

The Central Statistics Office collects information on the economic structure of each county which is not available for other regional divisions. Two such pieces of information provide the basis for the statistical measurement of location patterns. First, it is possible to ascertain the percentage of all industrial workers in each county. This is done simply by dividing the number of industrial workers in each county by the number of industrial workers in all counties. The resultant set of figures will be referred to here as the regional distribution of all industry. Second, it is possible to derive the percentage of each industry's employment which occurs in each county by dividing the number of workers occupied in an industry in each county by the total number of workers in the industry.

If a county contained, say, 4 per cent of all industrial employment it should, on assumption of perfect equality, also contain 4 per cent of the employment of every industry. This, of course, rarely happens. But if it held for one industry then the regional distribution of the industry in question would be coincidental with the regional distribution of all industry. Such an industry is said to be evenly scattered or dispersed. It has no localisation. A general definition may therefore be formulated: *the less a particular industry's distribution deviates from the distribution of all industry, the lower the industry's level of localisation.*

On the other hand, suppose there is a county with 4 per cent of total industrial employment which accounts for total (national) employment *in one industry*. It is easily seen that such an industry's regional distribution is significantly different from that of all industry. The industry is highly localised or highly concentrated in a specific region. Again, a summary definition follows: *the more the regional distribution of a particular industry differs from the distribution of all industry, the higher the industry's level of localisation.*

An important point emerges from the above discussion. In assessing the degree of localisation in an industry, the comparative yardstick is the regional distribution of all industry. This, however, is not a fixed datum and is likely to vary from year to year. It follows, then, that the concept of localisation is a relative concept. The index which measures it is called the *coefficient of localisation.* In the words of Florence it measures the 'local concentration of an industry compared with the distribution of industries as a whole'.(1) The index for a specific industry is derived as follows: select any region (county) and subtract the percentage of the industry's employment for which it accounts from the percentage of all industrial workers employed in the county. Repeat this operation for each region. Finally, sum all the negative (or positive) deviations and divide by 100. It can be seen that the total of positive deviations is equal to the total of negative deviations. This is necessarily so since the sets of figures whose deviations are measured total 100 per cent.

A few words should be said about the values the coefficient may assume. If an industry is distributed in the same way as all industry the coefficient is zero. Low values of the index indicate industries which conform closely to the general distribution of all industry, and consequently have little localisation. Increasing values of the coefficient reflect increasing regional concentration of the industry. In the extreme case, an industry which is located entirely in a specific region is denoted by a coefficient approaching unity.

The coefficient of localisation is a summary measure. It shows the degree of concentration or dispersion of any industry over all regions. However, it provides no information concerning the actual regions in which concentration occurs. To meet this need, a second index, called a *location quotient,* is used. It is found simply for each region by dividing the regional percentage of workers in the particular industry by the corresponding figure for all industries. It shows the number of times an industry's concentration in a region is greater than (less than) the over-all concentration of industry there.

A word of caution is appropriate concerning the interpretation of coefficient of localisation and location quotients. They are not absolute measures of regional concentration, but must be interpreted with reference to the regions in which the industry is located. For example, 20 per cent of the workers in all industry are employed in Dublin County Borough. Accordingly, in the case of an industry which is 100 per cent concentrated in Dublin, the location quotient may not be greater than 5 while the coefficient of localisation may not exceed 0·80. On the other hand, similar concentration in Longford containing just over 1 per cent of all industrial workers would yield indices of 100·00 and 0·99.

A third concept — geographical linkage — must now be introduced in order to measure the degree of relationship between two industries (e.g. metal trades and constructional engineering) or between two economic activities (e.g. bacon factories and pig production). There is a high degree of linkage between two industries if the regional distribution of employment in both corresponds closely. The strength of the linkage between industries is measured by a *geographical linkage coefficient*. It is similar in principle to the coefficient of localisation. However, instead of comparing the regional distribution of one industry with that of all industry, it compares the regional distribution of one industry with that of another. It is the sum of the negative (positive) deviations of the regional percentages of all workers in one industry from the corresponding regional percentages of all workers in the other industry divided by 100 and subtracted from unity.

1.3 Application of location measures to Irish industries

In the foregoing section, many references were made to 'an industry', but no definition was given. In theory, according to Stigler, 'an industry should embrace the maximum variety of productive activities in which there is strong, long-run substitution'. Thus. . . 'all products or enterprises with large, long-run cross elasticities of either supply or demand should be combined into a single industry'.[1]

[1]Quoted in Eveley and Little, *Concentration in British Industry*, (29).

What is theoretically desirable is rarely feasible in practice. From the theoretical viewpoint the ideal definition would refer to a collection of firms engaged in a single and similar economic activity. Even this, however, is not entirely satisfactory. Is an economic activity defined according to process (assembly), material used (steel), product (shirts), or service provided (insurance)? The situation is further confused by the fact that most firms engage in multiple activities. Product diversification within a firm or plant is more the rule than the exception. Very often the products are not even substitutes for each other, so that the activities carried out in many firms cut across the boundaries of a number of industries. Definitions must, therefore, sometimes be tailored to fit the information available. There are two main sources of information about Irish industries—the Census of Industrial Production and the Census of Population.[2] Industries are defined according to all four standards (i.e. process, product, material, and service) and assigned to three major categories: (i) mining, quarrying and turf production; (ii) manufacturing; and (iii) building, construction and service. The industry classification system used by the Central Statistics Office takes account of some elements of substitution (i.e. in so far as different items of confectionery, etc. may be considered substitutes for each other), but fails to take account of other elements (such as butter for margarine).

Coefficients of localisation and location quotients for each industry were derived from data appearing in Volume 4 of the 1961 Census of Population which provides a breakdown of each industry's employment on a county basis. The industry classification system used in the population census is not directly compatible with the system used in the Census of Industrial Production, nor is a complete reconciliation between the two possible. It is, however, possible to aggregate the major activities listed in the former to correspond with the classification system of the latter. One other source of discrepancy between the two is due to the fact that the population census covers all establishments while the census of production

[2] Cf. O'Mahony *The Irish Economy* (2) for a description and comparison of the contents of each.

covers only those establishments employing three or more persons. Thus, even if the census of industrial production gave a breakdown of each industry's employment on a regional basis, the location indices so computed would be less precise than indices based on the population census.

1.4 Table 1.1

TABLE 1·1

Coefficients of localisation for industries & services

	coefficient of local- isation		coefficient of local- isation
Building & construction	0·09	Bacon factories	0·49
Professions	0·10	Gas	0·50
Personal services	0·13	Glass, glassware, pottery & china	0·50
Commerce	0·13	Paints, vegetable & marine oils	0·50
Wood & cork	0·17	Rayon, nylon, cordage, jute etc.	0·53
Bread & flour confectionery	0·19	Distilling	0·53
Electricity	0·22	Ships and boats	0·54
		Repair & assembly; omnibuses & motor vehicles	0·54
Soft drinks	0·24		
Transport, communication & storage	0·26		
		Made up textiles	0·54
Public administration & defence	0·27	Pharmaceutical preparations, drugs & medicines	0·55
		Canned & preserved meats & other meat products	0·56
Insurance, banking & finance	0·29		
Metal products	0·29	Brewing	0·57
Grain milling & animal feedstuffs	0·30	Cocoa, chocolate & sugar confectionery	0·57
Miscellaneous food stuffs	0·37	Paper & paper products	0·57
Entertainment & sport	0·38	Boots & shoes	0·59
Structural clay products	0·38	Other vehicles	0·60
Hosiery & knitted goods	0·40	Shirts	0·61
		Electrical machinery & appliances	0·61
Leather & fur products	0·43		
		Canning of preserved fruit & vegetables	0·62
Furniture, brushes & brooms	0·44		
Machinery (except electrical etc.)	0·44	Tobacco	0·64
Dairy products	0·44	Malting	0·64
Woollen, worsted & carpets	0·46	Soap & candles	0·65
Clothing	0·47	Turf production	0·66
Fertilisers	0·48	Fellmongery	0·66
Mining & quarrying	0·48	Sugar	0·71
Printing & publishing	0·48	Locomotives	0·71
Linen, cotton & poplin	0·49	Biscuits	0·80

Coefficients of localisation for each industry are set out in Table 1.1. The general picture which emerges is one of an over-all tendency for the transportable goods industries to be highly concentrated. Twenty-five of the forty-five industries have coefficients of localisation (C.O.L.) greater than 0·50 while thirty-two industries have a C.O.L. greater than 0·45.

Not surprisingly, concentration occurs mainly in the Dublin region. If a location quotient greater than 1·00 is regarded as being indicative of some concentration, then only fourteen of either the forty-five transportable goods industries or the fifty-four listed activities do not show some concentration in Dublin. Moreover, eighteen of the transportable goods industries have location quotients greater than 2·00 for the Dublin region (see Appendix).

The food industries, however, are relatively unconcentrated in Dublin. Five of them (36·1 per cent) have location quotients greater than 2·00 for the Dublin region compared with thirteen of the remaining thirty-one industries (42 per cent). This has important economic consequences, the implications of which are examined in section 1·10.

Tables congested with figures give little information concerning the factors responsible for industry location. What is needed here is a series of hypotheses which are adequately substantiated by the facts. Certain industries will have similar location patterns because of the impact of similar forces. It is necessary, therefore, to classify industries according to some sets of common characteristics; for the present analysis three major divisions are used: (*i*) industries which are rooted to the sources of their material supplies; (*ii*) industries which are tied to the dispersion of their markets (residentiary industries) and (*iii*), industries which are 'footloose' i.e. tied neither to material supplies nor to the dispersion of their markets, and gravitate to the location of major markets.

1.5 Industries rooted to sources of material supplies

An industry is defined as being rooted to its sources of material supplies when it is located either in, or in close proximity to, those regions in which the raw materials it uses are found.

2

Eleven Irish industries fall into this category and they may be subdivided as follows:

(*a*) *extractive industries:* turf production, mining, and quarrying, cement and structural clay products;

(*b*) *food industries:* bacon, beef and mutton, dairy products, grain-milling and animal feeding stuffs, malting and sugar refining;

(*c*) *other industries:* fertilisers, assembly of mechanically propelled land and road vehicles.

What are the common characteristics of these industries? First, with the exception of the last mentioned, they are all continuous processing industries. That is, 'industries in which the operations to change the raw materials into finished products are performed in a continuous manner on the entire mass of materials.'(1) Second, a large number rely on one major material input (i.e. peat in turf production, pigs in bacon factories, cattle in beef production, barley in malting, milk in dairy products, sugar beet in sugar refining). On the other hand, in assembly industries, constituent parts of the product are manufactured simultaneously (perhaps in different industries) and then assembled. Thus, the wider range of materials or subproducts used in assembly industries will mean that even if they are supply-oriented, they will not be 'rooted' to a particular input to the same extent as continuous-processing supply-oriented industries. Third, the raw materials for the extractive industries are immovable. And finally, net output constitutes no more than 25 per cent of the gross output of the food industries. This is considerably lower than comparative figures for other industry groups. Thus, the relatively small value added per unit of output means that material costs constitute a high proportion of both total costs and gross output. This is particularly true in the case of the supply oriented food industries.(3)

What are the factors which have caused these industries to be supply-oriented? The answer may be found by analysing the relationship between the total cost of a product and the proportion of cost attributable to transport.

A product has three elements of cost: (*i*) the cost of transporting raw materials from their sources of supply to the plant of manufacture; (*ii*) the actual cost of processing at the plant and (*iii*), the cost of transporting the finished product to the market. The aim of a rational producer, obviously, is to minimise the total cost of production. Assume for the moment that the cost of processing is invariant to the location of the plant and that there is but a single material and a single market. Then total minimum cost is achieved when the plant is located in such a way as to minimise total transport costs. Whether this location is adjacent to the source of material inputs, the market, or at some point in between, will depend on the relative magnitude of the two elements of transport costs.

A few general rules may be laid down. If transport costs per unit of material input are very high or prohibitive, it is obvious that the plants of the industry will be located as close as possible to their sources of supply. This happens, of course, in the case of the extractive industries. It is also more likely to occur in industries in which material costs constitute a high proportion of gross output. For, since each unit of material input incurs a certain transport charge it follows that the more units of material input required per unit of output, the higher the total transport cost per unit of output.

One other feature of the supply-oriented industries is the bulkiness of the raw materials used. This increases transport costs on the supply side since transport rates are determined in part by the weight of the materials to be moved and the comparative ease or difficulty in handling them. The tendency to supply-orientation is reinforced if material inputs have a low value in relation to weight, and a high relative transport cost per unit weight of materials (dairy products, grain-milling); and if there is considerable loss of weight in the manufacturing process (bacon, beef and mutton, malting, sugar). Also, any combination of these factors for an industry in which the finished product has a relatively high value and a relatively low market transport cost is likely to lead to supply-orientation.

One other aspect of supply-orientation must be considered. An industry may use several material inputs. If the transport cost of materials is the basic consideration affecting location, then the industry may not be located in proximity to the sources of any one material input but rather in such a way as to minimise the total cost of hauling materials from several sources. However, as already seen, most of the supply-oriented industries in Ireland use a preponderance of a single material input. The degree to which some of them are 'rooted' to the sources of those materials is shown in Table 1.2.

TABLE 1·2

Linkage coefficients for the supply-oriented food industries & their main agricultural inputs

Linkage between	coefficient
Barley & grain milling	0·79
Barley & pigs	0·80
Wheat & grain milling	0·68
Wheat, oats, barley & grain milling	0·77
Bacon factories & pigs	0·79
Bacon factories & barley	0·76
Milk products & milch cows	0·70
Milk products & pigs	0·75
Milk products & bacon factories	0·71
Grain milling & milk products	0·70
Bacon factories & grain milling	0·73
Malting barley & malting	0·84
Sugar beet & sugar refining	0·82

The assumption that processing costs are invariant to the location of a plant can easily be relaxed. As far as supply-oriented industries are concerned, the transport cost of material is the overriding consideration. Thus, any saving of processing costs as a result of varying the location of the plant is offset by the increase in transport charges due to haulage of materials.

In conclusion, it should be noted that supply-oriented industries may assume any level of localisation. The degree to which they are concentrated or dispersed depends on the relative concentration or dispersion of material supplies. For example, turf production is highly localised (C.O.L. of 0·66) reflecting concentration of peat in Offaly and Kildare. On the other hand, dairy products (C.O.L. of 0·44) is a more dispersed industry due to the more dispersed distribution of milch cows.

1.6 Some features of particular supply-oriented industries

Fertilisers and motor assembly: These two industries differ from the other supply-oriented industries in that their raw materials are imported. Hence the necessity for their plants to be as close as possible to ports of entry. In the case of the fertiliser industry, the C.O.L. of 0·48 is due to the concentration of the industry in the major port regions (Dublin, Cork, Limerick, Waterford, Wicklow and Louth). The industry distribution is determined by the location pattern of channels through which raw materials are imported and the degree of localisation will depend on the number of such channels.(4) As regards motor assembly, the domination of transport considerations is due to the nature of the industry. It merely completes the final stage of production—the assembly of C.K.D. parts. These fulfill all qualifications regarding bulkiness, weight, difficulty in handling, etc.

Grain-milling and animal feeding stuffs: It is not possible to derive separate indices for the component sectors of this industry—flour milling and other mills, and manufacture of animal feeding stuffs. A characteristic of the latter is that, to a large extent, the farming sector is both the supplier of the raw materials and the market for the finished product. The Department of Agriculture Survey Team Report showed relative concentration in the south and eastern regions.(5) This locational structure is dictated by the concentration of barley growing in these areas, concentration of pig production and adjacency to ports. On the supply side there is a pull of two forces. On the one hand there are advantages in proximity to ports for the importation of maize, and on the other hand benefits accrue from proximity to the major barley growing areas. There is a geographical linkage coefficient of 0·80 between the distribution of barley acreage and pig numbers. This indicates a high correlation between the two activities and suggests that the best location for this industry is near inland supply areas.

Dairy products: This industry provides a good example of a location pattern determined by transport technologies. The location quotients indicate concentration in the south, particularly in the counties Cork, Limerick, Tipperary, Waterford and Kilkenny. The Department of Agriculture survey team found that 77 per cent of central creameries were situated in Munster, 8 per cent in Leinster, 8 per cent in Ulster and 7 per cent in Connacht. (6) However, despite the predominance of plants in Munster, the coefficient of localisation reveals only moderate concentration. This is due to the high dispersion of units within Munster itself. A multiplicity of plants owes its existence to the technologies employed in milk collection. The survey team found that 86 per cent of the suppliers in Munster providing 99 per cent of the milk, resided within four miles of the premises to which they supplied milk. In Limerick the corresponding proportion of suppliers was as high as 97 per cent. In contrast, the proportion was between 50 per cent and 60 per cent in Leinster, Ulster and Connacht. Seventy-eight per cent of all milk delivered was transported by producers themselves and the remainder was carted by haulage contractors or the creameries. It is not possible to say what effect bulk collection techniques would have on the location pattern of the industry as this would depend on the width of supply areas encompassed by the collection system and the transport costs involved in comparison with the location of market and the costs of distribution. However, it has been shown that transport innovations have tended to stimulate industry concentration. (7)

Bacon, and the beef and mutton industries: Location quotients for the bacon industry indicate nodal processing junctions at Cork and Limerick but particularly at Waterford with a quotient of 15·3. These quotients, however, overstate the actual concentration of the industry in these regions since they include employment in the beef, mutton, and lamb industry in the case of diversified plants in which pig and pigmeat production accounts for the major proportion of output. Similarly, location quotients listed for the canned and preserved meats industry embrace both units which are exclusively concerned with beef, mutton, and lamb production or in which such products account for the bulk of output. The downward bias in location quotients will, however, be much greater for the beef, mutton, and lamb industry since a higher proportion of diversified plants are primarily pigmeat oriented—41 per cent of bacon factories engage in beef processing while only 13 per cent of the beef and mutton factories engage in pig processing. The existence of the two industries in the same plant or locality is due to economies of agglomeration. Technically, both industries are of a complementary nature in production techniques, labour requirements and use of ancillary services. The bacon industry was established long before the development of the beef, mutton and lamb industry and in many cases diversification is merely the logical extension of the product mix, particularly since all units are engaged in the export of pig-meat products. Further-more, the widespread dispersion of cattle and sheep stocks in Ireland gives the beef, mutton, and lamb industry a 'footloose' character with respect to its supply base and facilitates its location in regions in which it may appropriate immobile internal and external economies. The high concentration of the industry in the Dublin/Kildare region is due to the immediate availability of beef cattle supplies and the advantages of proximity to Dublin in the case of an industry which exports the bulk of its output. (8)

1.7 Residentiary industries

Just as some industries may be rooted to the sources of material inputs because of the magnitude of material transport costs, others may be tied to their markets because of the cost of product distribution. In such cases the plants of an industry are located in a manner reflecting the distribution of the industry's market. The number of consumers each plant can serve is limited, hence the appellation 'residentiary.' The size of local or regional markets is determined by the width of the economic transport area for product distribution.

Industries falling into this classification include those in which products have a low value in relation to weight, a high or restrictive cost of distribution due to low portability or durability, and also products which gain considerable weight in the process of manufacture. The industries in the service sector and the building and construction trades conform to this pattern and their coefficients of localisation reveal wide-spread dispersion. Of the transportable goods industries only two—soft drinks, and bread and flour—may be regarded as being tied to the dispersion of the general population, while the wood and cork industry is closely linked to the building trades (the coefficient of geographical linkage is 0·80).

The terms 'exports' and 'imports' are generally used to describe the movement of goods and services between countries. However, they may also be applied in connection with the movement of products between different regions of the same country. For example, an industry in Dublin which serves markets in Kerry, Cork, or Galway 'exports' its products. Industries which export their output in this manner are called 'basic' or 'autonomous' industries while industries which do not engage in regional export are regarded as 'induced' activities. Since residentiary industries are confined to the service of local markets they are in fact 'induced' industries.

It has been shown that exports out of a region for a partticular industry tend to vary in the same direction as the regional location quotient, so that the higher an industry's regional location quotient, the higher its level of regional export activity. (9) Second, the demand for the products of a residentiary industry is closely related to the demand for the products of the export industries of a region.(10) Finally, it appears that any given increase in employment in basic industries will induce an even greater increase in secondary employment.(11) A study of regional employment patterns in Ireland by Baker concluded that 'in a particular year the relative size of the induced sector in a county seems to depend on the relative sizes of the non-agricultural autonomous sectors'.(12)

The data to hand appear to support Baker's findings since there is a correlation of 0·71 between the proportion of the total occupied population in each county engaged in autonomous industries and the proportion engaged in induced industries.[3] This strongly suggests that increases in the former will lead to an increase in the latter. There is, in fact, a multiplier effect since the expansion of employment in the service

[3]Employment in the autonomous sector was derived by subtracting the employment in the transportable goods industries defined as being induced from total employment in transportable goods industries. Total induced employment was then derived by subtracting this figure from total employment in economic activities (excluding agriculture). Accordingly, the present definitions of induced and autonomous activities are much less precise than Baker's.

industries leads to an increase in demand for the services themselves. The total income of a region, like that of a country,
depends on the volume of goods and services produced. Hence,
the greater the output of a region the larger its market size
whether defined in terms of total or per capita income. Thus
an increase in the concentration of an industry in a region
increases aggregate income and market size not only directly
but, more importantly, indirectly through its effect on the
demand for the output of residentiary industries.

1.8 Industries which gravitate to the location of major markets

There is no shortage of statistics reflecting high concentration
of industry in Dublin. Dublin has 44 per cent of the employment of all transportable goods industries. (Table 1.3) In the
case of eighteen of these industries location quotients are greater
than 2·0 indicating that Dublin accounts for at least 54 per
cent of their employment. Other pockets of industry concentration, though on a much more limited scale, may also be
found in Cork, Limerick and Waterford (especially in the
boroughs). With the exception of Dublin, only one other
county—Louth—has over 4 per cent of industrial employment;
two counties have between 3 per cent and 4 per cent, five
counties between 2 per cent and 3 per cent and sixteen under
2 per cent.

Location quotients for the western counties show the sparsity
of their economic activity. For example, only 17 transportable
goods industries operate in Leitrim. Of these, five have location
quotients which are less than 0·40 and regional exports would
appear to be negligible. As far as the other counties are concerned, the number of industries showing any degree of regional
concentration is few. Indeed, for the province of Connacht, as
a whole, only two industries—sugar, and linen and cotton—
have location quotients greater than 1·00.

This picture of an imbalanced industrial structure prompts
two questions: first, what factors are responsible for high
localisation? And, second, why is Dublin the main region of
concentration?

TABLE 1·3

Income and population statistics 1960 & 1961

	personal income by county as % of total income	county pop. as % of total pop.	county income per head as % of Dublin income per head	% of total economic activity (em.)	transportable goods industries	
					% em.	% em. other than food supply
Dublin	29·12	25·22	100·00	26·27	43·8	47·20
Carlow	1·27	1.18	93·07	1·11	1·0	0·61
Kildare	2·60	2·28	98·27	2·18	2·6	2·54
Kilkenny	2·40	2·20	94·81	2·14	1·6	1·38
Laois	1·64	1·61	88·31	1·61	1·2	1·06
Longford	0·94	1·10	73·59	1·07	0·4	0·47
Louth	2·15	2·39	77·92	2·43	4·5	4·91
Meath	2·57	2·31	96·10	2·29	1·7	1·86
Offaly	1·83	1·82	86·58	1·87	2·5	2·57
Westmeath	1·92	1·87	88·31	1·80	2·8	3·09
Wexford	2·76	2·97	80·09	2·81	1·6	1·46
Wicklow	2·11	2·07	87·88	2·00	1·9	2·05
Clare	2·20	2·63	72·29	2·65	1·0	0·93
Cork	11·66	11·71	86·15	11·64	12·8	11·96
Kerry	3·63	4·15	75·32	3·84	1·7	1·44
Limerick	4·85	4·73	88·31	4·39	3·4	2·54
Tipperary	4·67	4·41	91·77	4·25	3·2	2·54
Waterford	2·78	2·54	94·37	2·50	2·8	2·44
Galway	4·77	5·33	77·06	5·42	1·8	1·73
Leitrim	1·01	1·21	72·29	1·31	0·3	0·28
Mayo	3.40	4.42	66·23	4·45	1·4	1·30
Roscommon	1·81	2·12	73·59	2·25	0·6	0·58
Sligo	1·67	1·91	75·32	1·93	1·1	0·95
Cavan	1·67	2·04	71·00	2·14	0·8	0·75
Donegal	3·12	4·08	66·23	3·87	2·3	2·40
Monaghan	1·49	1·70	75·76	1·77	1·0	0·96
Total	100·00	100·00	—	100·00	100·00	100·00
	1960	1960	1960	1961	1961	1961

Hoover's analysis of the problem argues that regional concentration of industry is due to the economies of urban concentration of which there are three types: (*a*) *internal economies of scale*, i.e. 'large scale economies within a firm consequent upon the enlargement of the total output of that firm at that location; (*b*) *localisation economies* for all firms in a single industry consequent upon the enlargement of the total output of that industry at that location, and, (c) *urbanisation economies* for all firms in all industries consequent upon the enlargement of the total economic size (population, income, output or wealth) of that location'. (13)

Internal economies of scale arise from the advantage of bulk handling, specialisation of labour and machinery, spreading of overheads etc. The opportunity to exploit internal economies of scale is a powerful inducement for the individual firm to concentrate its production in a single plant in preference to several plants in different locations. While there may be an increase in either material transport costs or distribution costs, or both, such increases are outweighed by the cost reductions gained.

The second category of economies mentioned by Hoover was *localisation economies*. They refer to cost savings arising from the close physical association of several plants engaged in similar activities. Many of these economies, which are sometimes called immobile external economies, are of the same type as economies of scale. The more important, however, are of a different character and involve a particular relationship which may exist between the firms of a specific industry or among firms in different industries. They introduce the concept of direct producer interdependence which plays a significant role in many branches of economic theory, particularly development economics.

Most industries do not manufacture their own raw materials but purchase them instead from other industries. Thus the output of one industry becomes the input of another industry. An industry which is an 'input producer' may well be the 'output user' of a third industry. Thus a process of direct interdependence exists among industries and extends through the whole chain of interlocking industrial fabrications until those industries are reached which sell their output only to the general public and which are consequently designated final demand industries.

If the plants of an industry are concentrated in a specific location then other industries supplying input requirements can take advantage of large scale production to exploit internal economies—an opportunity that might not be realised if the plants of the input-using industry were more dispersed. The input using industry benefits from this situation since it will obtain material inputs at lower unit cost. Moreover, the proximity of both input-producing and output-using plants allows for lower transport costs which cause further cost reductions.

A second set of localisation economies is associated with the opportunities for specialisation. While plants in different industries may be related to each other as output users and input producers, specialisation may lead to a similar relationship among the plants of a single industry. Instead of engaging in a large number of fabricating or processing activities, each plant can specialise in particular functions. As Florence has pointed out, this is possible since 'the physical distance through which goods must pass from one special process to another may not be much greater from door to door than under the expanse of one roof'.(1) Even if transport costs are higher they are offset by the cost savings realised through specialisation. Furthermore, adjacency of plants also facilitates product specialisation since buying agents requiring full product lines do not incur significantly higher transport costs.

Localisation economies in the third set are more general. Firms in an industry use similar services such as machine repair and maintenance facilities, advertising, component parts, buying and selling agents. When the majority of firms are located in the same region the growth of specialised lower cost agencies to undertake these tasks is encouraged. In addition, firms can make arrangements to co-ordinate their buying and selling activities in order to take advantage of economies due to bulk handling. Other economies inducing localisation are the availability of a common labour supply, opportunities for mutually sponsored schemes for the training of labour, easier communications between producers with common interests and the fostering of an environment favourable to the growth of the industry.

Economies in the final category—*urbanisation economies*—are a further elaboration of localisation economies. Industries which are neither rooted to their material supplies nor tied to the dispersion of the population, tend to gravitate to those regions which are already characterised by a high density of population and concentration of industry i.e. to their major markets. The factors responsible for the localisation of a single industry also create pressures for industries related to it as output users or input producers to become similarly concentrated. These agglomerative tendencies are strengthened as a region develops because as the intensity of industry concentration increases the region develops a pool of skilled resources, a better communication system to ease the flow of knowledge, a managerial class and a sophisticated transport network. The larger market area encourages specialisation while high levels of investment in social overhead capital such as port and air installations, power plants, roads, etc. create economies for existing firms and result in lower setting up costs for new firms vis-à-vis costs in other less developed regions.

As far as Dublin is concerned some special features reinforce its position as both the major market for industry and centre of economic activity. First, population is concentrated in Dublin and the eastern counties. Dublin alone contains over one-quarter of the total population, has the highest per capita income and accounts for almost 30 per cent of total income. (Table 1.3) Leinster has a population equal to that of Munster and Connacht combined, and absorbs more than half of total income. Indeed, the disparity in income levels within the country is also apparent from Table 1.3 which shows that per capita incomes in Donegal and Mayo are only 66 per cent of that in Dublin. Second, Irish industries manufacture, for the most part, final demand products so that close proximity to the major centres of population is advantageous for the reasons already outlined. Perhaps most important, however, is the fact that most industries are highly dependent on imported raw materials and components.(14) For these industries and any industry which engages in export activity transport costs become a significant consideration.

Dublin, then, with its highly developed transport routes to all parts of the country and air and port facilities becomes, in the words of Hoover, a 'strategically placed transfer node with special locational advantages as a procurement and distribution point in the case of any activity for which transfer costs are important'.(13)

1.9 Some evidence of market-orientation among Irish industries

The reports of the survey teams established by the Committee on Industrial Organisation support the thesis that the impact of agglomeration economies coupled with the advantages of proximity to market have been the factors mainly responsible for the high concentration of industries in Dublin. Samples of their remarks in this regard are as follows:

Mantles and gowns: The factors influencing location have been 'availability of an ample labour force, particularly female labour, and the advantages of producing in the principal markets of the country where both buyers and final customers conglomerate'.(15)

Men's and boys' outerwear: 'Generally the tendency has been for this industry to develop in areas where industry has already developed... manufacturers prefer to operate in areas where there is a skilled pool of trained labour for which they must compete rather than in rural areas where they would have to train the operatives'.(16)

Toiletries: 'The products are usually small and of relatively high value, therefore transport costs are not a high proportion of sales, but these products are often demanded at short notice by retail outlets who keep only small supplies. To provide an efficient service for their principal markets the firms prefer to manufacture in or near large conurbations'. Other factors are intense competition and the use of personal sales techniques.(17)

Furniture: 'Furniture is bulky and liable to damage in transit... it is not the most suitable merchandise for carriage by rail. Proximity to market is accordingly an advantage and it is natural that Dublin should be the principal centre of the industry'.(18)

Paper and paper products: The technological requirement of a good water supply led to the concentration of the paper industry in Dublin.[4](14) In the case of the paper products sector, the report noted its important service function as supplier of packaging and containers to other industries, hence its concentration in the zone of major industrial activity.(19)

[4]It could therefore be argued that this section of the industry is supply-oriented.

Printing and publishing: 'Concentration of the industry in Dublin is largely due to the fact that Dublin has throughout been the administrative centre of the country and that a great amount of other industry has been established there.' Other reasons given are: proximity to the paper-mills, advantages in importing raw materials and facilities for training apprentices and servicing plant and equipment.(20)

Canning of fruit and vegetables: 'In view of the fact that the large vegetable processors rely on fresh home-grown produce to only a limited extent and that Dublin county is a source of supply of fresh ingredients we doubt whether they suffer any serious disability as a result of their location, having regard to their pattern of production. Moreover, any diseconomies on the supply side would be offset by the advantage of proximity to the major market—Dublin. However, if a processing plant were to concentrate on the processing of fresh home-grown produce, Dublin would not be the best location'.(21) Erin foods, of course, does, and accordingly is supply-oriented. However, its employment pattern is not included in the location quotients since they are based on 1961 data.

Distilling and brewing: It is pointless to ascribe the location pattern of these industries to any single factor. Since there are only nine establishments in the distilling trade, and eight in brewing (one of which is a giant firm), no rigid conclusion about location patterns can be drawn.

1.10 Inter-industry relationships

In section 1.8 the role of inter-industry relationships as a factor promoting localisation was emphasised. Altogether, four types of inter-industry linkages may be distinguished: (*i*) vertical linkages such as non-ferrous refining and non-ferrous wares; (*ii*) convergent linkages such as rivets and bolts which feed the assembly lines of other local industries such as railway carriages and motor vehicles; (*iii*) diagonal linkages such as construction engineering, foundries and other metal processes which service a number of local industries and (*iv*), more indirect social relations.(4) Accordingly, a geographical linkage coefficient computed in the manner described in section 1.2

may be explained in terms of either one or any combination of these four relationships.

From the standpoint of economic development, the concept of linkage which takes account of the direct interdependence of industries as output users and input producers is by far the most important. Such interdependence may be described as either backward linkage which establishes the degree to which the input requirements of one industry are provided through the domestic production of other industries or, forward linkage which measures the degree to which the output of one industry is used as inputs in other domestic industries.

Direct interdependence among producers stimulates economic growth in a number of ways. The benefits of innovations in one industry also accrue to many other industries, accelerating their growth, increasing their competitiveness and promoting higher levels of efficiency. The growth of one industry induces growth in all industries related to it as input producers. Such expansion may enable the firms in these industries to realise internal economies of scale. Resulting reductions in cost will be passed on, in the form of lower input prices, to all industries using their inputs. These industries in turn will realise lower costs which will also be passed on to industries using their outputs and so the process continues. There is then a continuous complex interaction among firms and industries which creates these 'dynamic external economies'. And it is for this reason that many economists suggest that underdeveloped countries establish 'poles of development', in other words, that they promote the establishment of those industries which induce considerable forward and backward linkage.

Production interdependence may also be viewed as a process of vertical disintegration. In this sense it is characterised by 'the progressive division and specialisation of labour'. However, the extent to which specialisation can occur is limited by market size. When an industry is small its total input and service requirements are not large enough to induce the entry of new firms which could supply them on a profitable basis. And as Stigler points out, 'young industries are often strangers to the established economic system. They require new kinds and qualities of raw materials and hence make their own. They must persuade customers to abandon other commodities and find no specialised merchant to undertake this task. These young industries must design their specialised equipment and often manufacture it, and they must undertake to recruit skilled labour'.(22) However, when an industry has reached a certain size its requirements of particular inputs can be supplied at competitive prices by other firms especially established for the purpose. With continued growth many other tasks can be farmed out to specialist agencies. Thus one can trace the way in which an industry vertically disintegrates into several component industries each one of which performs one stage of fabrication or one specialised service. In each instance the determinant of the degree to which this actually occurs is the level of demand. For in each sub-industry there is some minimum economic plant size which is defined by that level of output which enables a domestic firm to earn normal profits and to compete with foreign suppliers.(23) Unless demand in the 'master' industry for a specific component reaches this level vertical disintegration will not occur.[5]

It is for this reason that developing and underdeveloped countries tend to be characterised by industrial structures in which direct producer interdependence is largely absent. Industries, as a rule, are of the type which transform either primary products or imported semi-manufactures into final demand products. Irish industries conform closely to this pattern. As already pointed out, they rely heavily on imported materials and components, they cater almost exclusively for final demands and a number of reports point out their lack of specialisation and indeed stress their over-diversification.(14) It is reasonable, then, to conclude that industry localisation patterns and more specifically the high concentration of industry in Dublin has not been due to the external economies associated with direct producer interdependence but rather to internal economies of scale and the more general form of urbanisation economies.[6]

[5]Needless to say, these descriptions of direct interdependence and vertical disintegration are very limited in scope and take no account of the many obstacles which may hinder their effective operation.

[6]Statistical evidence supporting this conclusion is presented in Chapter 3 which investigates the relationship between location and plant size.

While it is possible, therefore, to derive high geographical linkage coefficients between any number of industries localised in Dublin their interpretative value is limited.

On the other hand a more rigorous analysis is possible in the case of the supply-oriented food industries and their geographical inter-relationships with each other and the sources of their principal agricultural inputs. In contrast to other industries, they are primarily dependent on the use of domestic raw materials. As a result the high linkage coefficients in Table 1.2 are attributable to direct interdependence between variegated forms of agricultural production and the respective processing industries. Because of the fact that transport costs are the overriding consideration affecting location, these industries must necessarily be located in alignment with the distribution of their material supplies.

Perhaps most important of all is the contribution the food industries have made to regional development. One prerequisite of economic development is the growth of manufacturing industry while developmental programmes usually give priority to a more efficient allocation of resources. But criteria of efficiency can often conflict with social considerations and must therefore be modified. It is generally accepted that interregional inequalities of growth are both an inevitable concomitant and a condition of growth itself.(23) The past experience of Ireland in this respect may be surmised from Table 1.4. It shows that the industrial structure is characterised by widespread and significant interregional inequalities in the distribution of manufacturing industry. But such inequalities would have been much worse were it not for the 'smoothing' influence of the supply-oriented food industries. Though the Dublin region absorbs 14 per cent of employment in these industries this represents only 3.2 per cent of Dublin's total employment. On the other hand the remaining 86 per cent of employment in the food industries accounts for over 20 per cent of industrial employment in eight counties and between 18 and 20 per cent in the case of a further two. (Table 1.4) Their contribution to employment is greatest in the south and south-eastern counties, which are, of course, those regions in which the agriculture-processing industry linkage complex is

TABLE 1·4

Regional employment in the food industries as % of transportable goods industries regional employment (1961)

County	A supply-oriented industries[a]	B industries tied to markets[b]	market oriented industries[c]	total
Dublin	3·2	4·2	15·0	22·4
Carlow	45·2	8·9	0·7	54·8
Kildare	11·8	3·0	3·6	18·4
Kilkenny	23·5	5·6	6·8	35·9
Laois	20·0	2·0	3·4	25·4
Longford	3·9	7·8	0·2	11·9
Louth	2·4	3·8	3·0	9·2
Meath	4·0	5·6	2·9	12·5
Offaly	7·3	2·9	1·9	12·1
Westmeath	1·1	2·6	0·6	4·3
Wexford	20·0	7·7	2·6	30·3
Wicklow	2·9	4·3	4·8	12·0
LEINSTER	5·4	4·3	11·1	20·8
Clare	14·3	5·3	1·4	21·0
Cork	16·0	6·0	5·8	27·8
Kerry	23·8	9·0	3·1	35·9
Limerick	32·2	7·2	3·2	42·6
Tipperary	28·0	7·1	4·8	39·9
Waterford	23·0	6·0	3·8	32·8
MUNSTER	21·0	6·5	4·7	32·2
Galway	12·1	10·4	5·9	28·4
Leitrim	12·2	9·3	4·5	26·0
Mayo	18·8	8·3	1·5	28·6
Roscommon	10·0	5·1	2·3	17·4
Sligo	19·6	8·5	2·5	30·6
CONNACHT	15·3	8·7	3·5	27·5
Cavan	19·0	4·4	2·5	25·9
Donegal	7·0	6·3	3·6	16·9
Monaghan	12·4	4·2	2·7	19·3
ULSTER (part of)	10·7	5·4	3·2	19·3
Total	10·0	5·1	8·8	23·9
Total (excl. Dublin)	15·4	5·8	3·8	25·0

(a) Bacon factories, canned & preserved meats, sugar, malting, grain milling & milk products.

(b) Bread & flour confectionery, soft drinks.

(c) Canning of fruit & vegetables, brewing, distilling, cocoa, chocolate & sugar confectionery, biscuits & miscellaneous food preparations.

most dominant. While it is impossible to evaluate completely the impact of this linkage on the growth of these regions some estimate of its past contribution can be gleaned from Table 1.3. The dominant counties in the complex have relatively high per capita incomes, particularly Waterford, Limerick and Tipperary. Also, those counties with the highest proportions of their industrially employed in the supply-oriented food industries tend to account for higher proportions of other industrial employment (with the exception of Dublin and counties on the periphery). Thus, by creating an industrial environment and a concomitant social overhead infrastructure the linkage has helped to attract other industry into these regions.

Indeed, all of the food industries have played an important role in counterbalancing to some extent the concentration of industry in Dublin. In three counties they account for over 40 per cent of industrial employment and for 33 per cent or more in the case of five others. Only in nine counties do they fail to account for at least one-fifth of industrial employment.

1.11 Conclusion

The dominant feature of the locational structure of Irish industry is the high concentration in the Dublin region. Contributary factors have been; (a) the nature of industry: of the 45 listed transportable goods industries, only 12 can be regarded as being primarily tied to particular location patterns because of either material supply or market considerations; (b) the high dependency of industry on imported raw materials and components coupled with the advantages of Dublin as a transport network with respect to both the domestic and export markets; (c) economic factors: the scope to realise internal economies of scale and urbanisation economies encourages firms to concentrate their production in a specific location; (d) demographic features and distribution of markets: not only is the total population of Ireland small in absolute terms but population density is also low. Population is concentrated in Dublin and the eastern counties. In addition, regional per capita incomes vary significantly, being as low in some counties as 66 per cent of the level in Dublin.

Regional inequalities of income levels may arise because of

low productivity per head in all industries of a region caused by a high proportion of low productivity industries. Social objectives in a region may include policies to relieve hardship and congestion. But in the long-term the economic development of that region will depend on the integration of regional development plans into an over-all national programme.

One of the aims of such programmes must be the attraction of new industries into a region. Some relevant considerations are as follows:

(1) Since Dublin is both the main port and the main centre of domestic purchasing power it has many agglomerative advantages. Some of these arise from the fact that it is the rational location of any market-oriented industry, the more so if it exports some of its products and/or imports a major portion of its raw materials. It may be argued, therefore, that if other ports were adequately developed (e.g. Waterford, Cork) some of Dublin's pull for market-oriented industries with significant exports would diminish. This could affect the market-oriented food industries, especially as any major expansion of these must be for export purposes.

(2) Industry can only be attracted successfully into a region if its efficiency is not adversely affected by location structure. Accordingly, given the regional characteristics of the supply-oriented industries, a case can be made for promoting their expansion more vigorously than the expansion of other industries, which have to or tend to, be located in Dublin.

(3) Continued expansion of the economy will at some time result in the growth of direct producer interdependence. Given the present pattern of industry distribution it is reasonable to assume that this process will reinforce the tendency for industry to concentrate in Dublin.

(4) There is little point in encouraging the establishment of residentiary industries, since they are basically induced activities and are an effect rather than a cause of development. Moreover, the degree to which industries are residentiary is a function of the state of their existing technology. In the case of

the bread and flour industry and the soft drinks industries, it is possible, indeed probable, that their residentiary character will weaken due to changes in their technologies. This would be aggravated by innovations in transport, storage and container techniques.

2 THE STRUCTURE OF INDUSTRY PLANT SIZES

2.1 Introduction

Very often the picture drawn of highly developed economies is one of mammoth business empires with bigness associated with efficiency. Poorer countries, on the other hand, are typified as having a lack of business organisation, an inadequate capital structure and a proliferation of small, inefficient plants. Smallness, and the supposed shortcomings it entails, are ascribed in part to the limitation of market size. This argument is succinctly summarised by Scitovosky who writes that 'at a given set of factor prices a given output can be produced by several methods of production entailing different production costs. The rate of output that minimises unit costs of production is likely to be different for each method the higher the rate of output needed to reach minimum per unit costs or the larger the optimum size of the plant. In a limited market the producer is faced with a falling demand curve for his product and rising supply curve for his factors. The price charged depends upon the output to be marketed and if the more efficient method requires a higher rate of output for the full exploitation of their economies, then the output obtained by these methods is likely to be sold at a lower price. This disrupts the correspondence between profitability and efficiency because it lowers the profitability of the more efficient methods relative to that of less efficient ones. Hence the possibility that the limits to the entrepreneur's markets may render unprofitable the adoption and use of the more capital intensive methods of production.' (24)

A number of questions spring to mind. How does one measure plant size? Is it meaningful to typify an industry as having small plants or large plants? What would be revealed by a comparison between the plant structures of individual Irish industries and those of a developed economy such as Britain?

What relative differences exist among the plant structures of Irish industries? And finally, what factors determine plant sizes in an industry? These questions, with the exception of the last, are discussed in this chapter. The final question then becomes the topic of Chapter 3.

2.2 The measurement of plant size

It is not unusual for the economist to catalogue the short-comings of a model or technique and then to go straight ahead and use it. This is very apparent in the measurement of plant size. Ideally a measure should correspond to the concept of economic capacity. But this has been defined, at different times, in terms of the outputs at which a firm's average cost curve becomes vertical, at which average cost is minimised and at which marginal revenue and marginal cost are equal. This raises considerations of the short run and the long run, ambiguities concerning ideal output, actual output and what constitutes excess capacity due to the imperfections of competition. Thus, besides the enormous, and in most cases insuperable difficulties of assembling the necessary data, even for a few plants, the problems of processing and interpretation mean that economic capacity is not a viable empirical measure of plant size.

While alternative measures e.g. of employment, output or capital suffer from even more interpretative drawbacks and are far less precise, they are at least capable of being computed. Average number of employees per establishment is probably the most popular measure of plant size. However, since most industries contain a large number of plants accounting for a small proportion of employment and a small number of plants accounting for a high proportion, a mere arithmetic average of such skewed distributions may be very misleading if no weight is attached to different size categories. They may provide a reasonable basis for inter-industry comparisons as long as distributions are similar in the countries being compared. (25) The argument for using gross output rather than employment centres on the contention that in large plants output per head is normally high due to the substitution of capital for labour. Indeed, disparities between measures of plant size based on output and measures based on employment are frequently found in empirical research. An analysis of British and American industries showed that the use of average employment per plant did not reveal significant differences in the plant size structure in the two countries, while in terms of output per plant U.S. plants were two and a half to three times as big as their British counterparts. (26) But output as a measure of size is equivocal in international comparisons, especially if the industry's output is heterogeneous: aggregation introduces a bias into the measure. When output is measured in monetary terms further complications arise on account of currency exchange rates and variation in price levels and living standards. Besides, a simple average of output per plant is open to the same criticism as employment per plant. Finally, capital indices as a measure of size are advocated on the grounds that employment is only one determinant of capacity and that employment measures of size result in a downward bias in the case of capital-intensive industries or industries substituting capital for labour. While these propositions may very well be valid, they are more than offset by the problems posed by the theoretical and operational definition and measurment of capital.

It seems, then, that of the alternatives open, some variant of the employment measure would prove least inadequate, especially if there were a way of weighting the importance of different size classes within an industry. A technique embodying this approach was developed and used by Florence. He argued that '. . . if a typical size of plant is to be discovered in any industry what is wanted as a measure is the size from which a certain bulk of the output of that industry comes. A majority of plants might be, and in most industries in fact are, of small size but their very smallness means that their aggregate output is small and of little importance in the output of the whole industry.[1] Physical outputs cannot be compared in a common measure but statistics of men employed may be used as a rough

---

[1]This is also true of Irish industry. In 1958, 50 per cent of establishments employing 15 persons or less accounted for only 7 per cent of gross output. Only 9·8 per cent of establishments were employing 100 persons or over and yet this category accounted for 64 per cent of gross output and over 66 per cent of net output. (25)

index of size of output per plant. Hence, to find what sizes of plants provide the bulk of output, we may inquire into what consecutive sizes the bulk, say 50 per cent of wage-earners are employed.' (1)

Thus the concept of prevalent plant size in an industry requires that some size-classes measured in terms of employment be regarded as being representative of the industry as a whole. They must therefore contain the majority of the industry's employment. The normal rule is that two adjacent size classes should contain at least 50 per cent of the industry's employment. For example, 30 per cent of employment in the bacon industry occurs in plants employing between 100 and 199 persons and a further 48 per cent occurs in plants employing 200–499 persons. These two size-classes are adjacent and between them they account for over 50 per cent of employment. It is now possible to assign a definite plant size grade by consulting the rules set out in Table 2.1. They indicate

TABLE 2·1

Rules for the assignment of industries to plant size categories

Grade of size	Florence classification		Irish classification	
	percentage of total persons employed	*in establishments employing*	*percentage of total persons employed*	*in establishments employing*
Small Plant	50	less than 50	50	less than 30
	60	less than 100	60	less than 50
Smallish plant	50	50–199	50	30–99
	60	25–199	60	20–99
Medium	50	100–499	50	100–499
Largish plant	50	500–1,000	50	200–499
Large plant	50	1,000 or more	50	500 or more
Bias towards small plant	60	under 200	60	under 200
Bias towards large plant	75	over 200	50	over 200

that medium size plants typify the bacon industry. If no two consecutive class intervals add up to 50 per cent the industry is regarded as having no prevalent plant size. However, since size-classes are of a small range at the lower end of the scale this rule is modified so as to qualify industries with 60 per cent of their workers in the size-classes specified in Table 2.1 for a prevalent plant size rating.

The application of the Florence rules to Irish industries yields valid measures of plant sizes for a comparison with British industries. But since the rules were designed for a highly industrialised country they are apt to conceal relative differences in the plant size structure of Irish industries. A second classification system was used therefore in order to take account of this factor (Columns. 4 and 5 of Table 2.1). The only significant changes which occur concern some industries which have medium plants on the Florence scale and which are now assigned to the large or largish size category.[2]

The basic data for Irish industries was published in the Supplement to the 1960 Census of Industrial Production. Because of the need to conceal the identity of particular firms the Central Statistics Office is obliged to lump size categories in the case of some industries.[3] The plant size structure of British industries is well documented by Florence. The size gradings used in this study were derived from his publication *Post-War Investment Location and Size of Plant* (27)

2.3 Plant size structure of Irish industries on Florence scale

Details of the prevalent plant sizes assigned to Irish industries on both the Florence and Irish scales are set out in the following table.

A definite plant size was assigned to 37 of the 44 industries listed. Although more than half of these were assigned to the medium or larger plant size categories it is evident from Table 2.3 that in terms of output and employment the small plant

[2]Largish plants are now assigned to the size grade 200–499. While some of the C.I.O. reports regarded firms employing over 200 employees as being large, a cross-industry application of this standard would conceal significant differences in industry plant sizes.

[3]Cf. O'Malley *The structure and performance of Irish industry 1953–63* (3) for a description of the methods and assumptions used to obviate these lumpings.

TABLE 2·2

Classification of industries according to prevalent plant size

Industry	Florence size classification	Irish size classification
FOOD:		
Bacon factories	Medium	Largish
Slaughtering etc. of other meat	Medium	Largish
Milk products	Small	Small
Canning of fruit & vegetables	Medium	Largish
Grain milling	Small	Bias to small
Bread, biscuits & flour confect.	N.P.S.	N.P.S.
Sugar	Bias to large	Largish
Cocoa, choc. & sugar confect.	N.P.S.	Largish
Misc. food preparations	Small	Small
DRINK & TOBACCO:		
Distilling	N.P.S.	Medium
Malting	Small	Small
Brewing	Large	Large
Aerated & mineral waters	Small	Small
Tobacco	Largish	Large
TEXTILES:		
Woollen & worsted	Medium	Medium
Linen & cotton	Medium	Medium
Jute, canvas, rayon, nylon	Largish	Large
Hosiery	Medium	Medium
Made up textile goods	Small	Smallish
CLOTHING & FOOTWEAR:		
Boots and Shoes	Medium	Medium
Clothing	Small	Bias to small
Shirt making	Small	Smallish
WOOD & FURNITURE:		
Manufacture of wood & cork	Small	Small
Furniture, brushes and brooms	Small	Small
PAPER & PRINTING:		
Paper & paper products	N.P.S.	N.P.S.
Printing & publishing	N.P.S.	N.P.S.
CHEMICALS:		
Fertilisers	Bias to small	Bias to small
Oils, paints, inks & polishes	Small	Bias to small
Chemicals & drugs	Small	Smallish
Soaps, detergents, candles	N.P.S.	Largish

TABLE 2·2—*continued*

Classification of industries according to prevalent plant size

Industry	Florence size classification	Irish size classification
CLAY PRODUCTS:		
Glass, pottery, earthenware	Bias to large	Largish
Structural clay & cement	Bias to small	Bias to small
METAL & ENGINEERING:		
Metal trades	Smallish	Bias to small
Machinery (except electrical)	Small	Small
Electrical machinery	N.P.S.	Bias to large
Ship building & repairs	Bias to large	Largish
Railroad equipment	Large	Large
Mechanically propelled vehicles	Bias to large	Bias to large
Assembly of other vehicles	Medium	Medium
OTHER INDUSTRIES:		
Leather goods	Small	Bias to small
Fellmongery	Medium	Largish
Building & construction	Small	Small
Mining & quarrying	Medium	Bias to largish
Turf production	Large	Large

industries are by far the most significant group. They alone
are responsible for almost 41 per cent of employment and 38

TABLE 2·3

Distribution of industries, net output & employment according to plant size classifications

Percentage distribution of	n.p.s.	small	small-ish	bias to small	total small	med-ium	bias to large	lar-gish	large	total large	total
Industries	15·9	34·0	2·3	4·5	40·8	22·7	9·1	4·5	6·8	20·4	100
Net output	22·5	30·2	3·9	3·5	37·6	18·4	6·2	4·7	10·6	721·5	100
Employment	22·6	34·7	3·9	2·3	40·9	20·2	5·7	3·3	7·3	16·3	100

N.P.S.=no prevalent plant size.

per cent of net output whereas the large plant industries account
for less than 22 per cent of output and employment. The

Florence scale shows, therefore, that the bulk of output and employment in Ireland is provided by industries in which the scale of organisation is small or medium.

This type of organisation is most prevalent in the three industry groups comprising clothing and shoes, wood and furniture and chemicals, while the textile group has a strong medium plant orientation. The overall effects of smallness are mitigated by three groups—metal and engineering, glass and clay products and the food industry. And of these, metal and engineering lays strong claims to being characterised by the relatively largest plant size structure. It accounts for the highest proportion of industries with large plant sizes, the lowest proportion of small plant industries and, with the exception of the glass and clay group, a higher proportion of its constituent industries have large plants.

2.4 Comparision of plant sizes in British and Irish industries

Prevalent plant size rankings for 26 more or less similar British and Irish industries have been established.[4] These industries account for over 60 per cent of net output and 69 per cent of employment, and are therefore reasonably representative of Irish industry as a whole.

Surprisingly enough, there seems to be an overall similarity in rankings. Twelve industries have a similar rank, four are one grade apart and six others are two grades apart. Only four industries reveal notable differences in size classifications (i.e. appear in one of the small size categories in one country and in the medium or larger categories in the other). But too much should not be read into this general picture of similarity. It is in fact, quite misleading, concealing as it does the differences in industry scale in both countries. The significance of scale is illustrated in Table 2.4 which shows for a number of industries the employment in the largest sized class intervals in Britain and total employment in similar industries in Ireland. Some features of this Table deserve comment. First, even in industries which are classified in the small plant category in both countries, employment in the British industry in the size-class

[4]*ibid.*

TABLE 2·4

Scale of British & Irish industries

| Industry | Britain | | Ireland | | plant size | |
| | largest size category | employment in largest size category | largest size category | total employment | Britain | Ireland |
					Florence Scale	
Woollen & worsted	1000–over	13,800	500–999	6046	medium	medium
Oils, paints, ink etc.	1000–over	4,700	100–199	1256	n.p.s.	small
Chemicals & drugs	1000–over	17,600	100–199	1527	n.p.s.	small
Machinery (excl. electrical)	1000–over	219,000	200–499	1476	largish	n.p.s.
Electrical machinery etc.	1000–over	177,200	500–999	3731	largish	small
Leather goods	200–499	1,921	100–199	665	small	bias to large
Ship building	1000–over	128,544	200–499	813	large	small
Dairy products	1000–over	3,200	200–499	4067	bias to small	medium
Canning of fruit & vegetables	1000–over	6,600	200–499	1983	n.p.s.	medium
Bacon factories	500–999	4,200	200–499	3905	small	medium
Fellmongery	200–499	10,700	200–499	1457	smallish	small
Wood & Cork	500–999	3,800	100–199	3545	small	small
Soft drinks	500–999	2,575	100–199	1524	small	bias to small
Cement & structural clay products	1000–over	2,800	200–499	2606	bias to small	n.p.s.
Soaps & candles etc.	1000–over	11,500	200–499	668	largish	bias to large
Glass & chinaware	1000–over	35,200	200–499	2374	bias to large	largish
Jute, canvas, rayon & nylon	1000–over	36,500	500–999	3225	n.p.s.	bias to small
Furniture, brushes & brooms	1000–over	4,400	100–199	3789	small	bias to small
Clothing	1000–over	29,100	200–499	13691	bias to small	small
Linen & cotton	1000–over	28,400	500–999	3490	medium	medium
Boots & shoes	1000–over	12,700	500–999	5349	medium	medium
Hosiery	1000–over	12,600	500–999	5323	n.p.s.	medium
Made up textiles	200–499	1,350	100–199	700	smallish	small

NOTE: Employment figures etc. for British industries refer to 1951. (14)

500–999 is usually greater than the total industry employment in Ireland (e.g. wood and cork, soft drinks). Second, Irish industries designated as having small plants generally have little or no employment in class intervals greater than 100–199. On the other hand similarly ranked British industries may have considerable proportions of their employment in size-classes of 500–999 and greater. Third, British industries with prevalent plant sizes smaller than their Irish counterparts often contain size-classes larger than the largest size-class in the industry here. Indeed, employment in these size-classes alone may exceed total employment in the Irish industry. The outstanding example of this occurs in the bacon industry. It is classified as a medium plant size industry in Ireland and as a small plant size industry in Britain. Even on the basis of average employment per plant, Irish plants are nearly twice as large. Yet, in Ireland there is no employment in the size-class 500–999 whereas in Britain this size category accounts for 18 per cent of employment containing 4,230 employees compared with the Irish industry's total employment of 3,905. Finally, Irish industries classified as having medium or larger plants have an upward bias compared with similarly ranked British industries. This is most apparent in the case of some of the textile trades and the metal and engineering group. For example, British woollen and worsted, linen and cotton and boots and shoes contain more employees in the size-classes 1,000 and over than total employment in the corresponding Irish industries. As far as the engineering etc. industries are concerned, one example will suffice to illustrate the difference in scale. Over 170,000 are employed in the size-class 1,000 and over in the British electrical machinery, appliances and apparatus industry. This figure exceeds total employment in Irish transportable goods industries in 1958.

The evidence then is clear: in absolute terms both the scale of British industry and the overall plant size structure are significantly larger than in this country.[5]

2.5 Conclusion

This chapter began an investigation into the relationships

[5]This confirms the findings of Linehan's study. (25)

between the prevalent size of plant in an industry and a number of other economic variables. It was found that in absolute terms both the scale of industry and the plant structure of different industries in Britain are significantly larger than in Ireland, but that in relative terms the plant size structure of comparable industries is remarkably similar in both countries. It appears, therefore, that the factors influencing the size structure of different industries are not peculiar to any one country but arise out of the nature of the industry itself.

3 LOCATION AND PLANT SIZE

3.1 Introduction

In economic theory plant size is determined by the desire of rational entrepreneurs to maximise profits. The scale of output in each firm is set at that level which results in the greatest difference between total costs and total revenues i.e. where marginal cost equals marginal revenue. Two types of profit maximising decisions are distinguished. In the short-run plant size is regarded as a fixed factor. An increase in demand can be met only by the more intensive use of the existing plant because the period is too short to allow for the construction of additional capacity. In the long-term, plant size as well as all other productive inputs are variable factors. The long-term is concerned with variations in the scale of operations which may yield economies or diseconomies of scale. It should be borne in mind at this point that entrepreneurs are not concerned with setting up plants which will enable them to produce most efficiently, that is to say at the miminum unit cost. Only under conditions of pure competition does it happen that profits are maximised when a firm is producing at its lowest average cost. In other more realistic market structures such as monopolistic competition, oligopoly and monopoly, this marriage of economic efficiency and maximum profitability does not occur.

The theory outlined does not provide a very satisfactory framework for the analysis of prevalent plant size in an industry. On a practical level existing plants must be regarded as embodying both long and short term features. The structure of an economic order is in a continuous state of evolution. Thus, in some industries many plants have been in operation over a long period and have adjusted through the years to changes in external factors such as demand, technology, etc., while other plants may be unable to re-organise due to shortage of invest-ment or other reasons. It is doubtful whether profit maximisa-tion is an exact description of the manner in which businessmen behave. It is hard to imagine them grappling with the im-ponderables involved in computing marginal revenues and marginal costs. On the other hand, it would be even more unreasonable to reject the role of profit in business decision-making or to deny the response of businessmen to profit-oppor-tunities. But while a businessman may seek a high level of profit this has nothing to do with profit maximisation. Moreover, as an answer to the question of what determines the prevalent size of plant in an industry, profit-motivation is inadequate. To say that some industries have small plants and others large plants because these structures are the most profitable in each instance does not add much to the store of knowledge. What is required is to show why it is more profitable for some industries to have large plants and others small plants. To do this it is necessary to examine the characteristics of industries and the nature of the activities they carry out in relation to their prevalent plant sizes. Such an investigation may lead to some conclusions about the determinants of industry plant structures. Industries have already been categorised according to location patterns and that analysis can now be taken one step further. This chapter therefore deals with the relationship between the location pattern of industries and their prevalent plant sizes.

3.2 Plant size and location

The relationship between the level of localisation in an industry and its prevalent plant size is summarised in Table 3.1. This table is quite easy to interpret. It shows, for example, that of the industries with a C.O.L. less than 0.30, 80 per cent have a small plant structure. Similarly, of those industries which are the most highly concentrated (C.O.L. greater than 0.60) 9 per cent have small plants, 9 per cent smallish, 9 per cent medium, 9 per cent bias to large 36 per cent largish and 27 per cent large. When the respective small and large size categories are aggregated in the manner shown in the last three columns of Table 3.1, three definite patterns emerge. First, industries with a low degree of localisation tend to have small

TABLE 3·1

Percentage of industries within each of the localisation groups

Coefficient of Localisation	small	smallish	bias to small	medium	bias to large	largish	large	no prevalent size	grouped		
									small	medium	large
0·0–0·29	80		20						100		
0·30–0·39	33		67						100		
0·40–0·44	60		20	20					80	20	
0·45–0·49				29	29	14	14	14	29	29	29
0·50–0·59		15	8	15	8	31	15	8	23	15	54
0·60–over	9	9		9	9	36	27		18	9	73

plants. Second, industries with moderate localisation (0.45–0.49) tend to have a heterogeneous structure of plant sizes. And finally, industries with a high level of localisation tend to have large plants. Moving from the top left hand corner of the last three columns to the bottom right it is clear that there is a strong linear relationship between plant size and degree of localisation which indicates that the higher the level of localisation in an industry the larger its prevalent plant size.

The data can also be examined in another light. Consider first the behaviour of residentiary industries. It will be recalled from Chapter 1 that they are characterised by low levels of localisation. A second characteristic can now be added: they are also typified by small prevalent plant sizes. (Tables 3.2)

TABLE 3·2

Contingency table of localisation and plant size for residentiary & supply-oriented industries

C.O.L. between	prevalent plant size		
	small	medium	large
Residentiary industries*			
0–0·29	100·0		
Supply-oriented industries			
0·30–0·44	100·0		
0·45–0·53	33·3		66·6
0·54–Over	20·0		80·0

*It was possible to compute plant size for the non-service residentiary industries only.

Now look at the supply-oriented industries. Those which are relatively dispersed (C.O.L. between 0·30 and 0·44) have small plant sizes, and as the level of localisation intensifies the proportion of industries with small plants diminishes while the proportion with large plants steadily increases.

It seems, then, that residentiary industries and supply-oriented industries rooted to dispersed material bases share two features: low levels of localisation and small plant sizes. The reason for this can be found in the domination of transport considerations. Dispersed supplies or scattered markets mean increases in transport costs per unit of input or output which would more than outweigh any saving in processing costs due to the internal economies of a larger plant. On the one hand the concentration of the industry cannot exceed that of its material-supply bases and on the other, the concentration of a residentiary industry cannot become greater than that of its markets. The important point is that among these industries prevalent plant sizes are the result of technical and physical constraints. The industries can only organise on a scale which reflects the ability of technology to overcome the economic handicaps imposed by the nature and location of the materials they use, the markets they serve, the process they perform and the product they manufacture. It is reasonable to believe that if in the 'long run' advances in technology ease the severity of these constraints, corresponding re-adjustments in plant size structure will occur in the industries concerned.

A somewhat similar argument applies to those supply-oriented industries with moderate and high localisation. Dispersed supplies no longer constitute a barrier to the scale of organisation. While the concentration of material inputs in particular regions narrows the range of optional locations, it increases the width of the economic transport area for each firm and thus opens the way for larger-scale production. Indeed, the highly localised supply-oriented industries and the highly localised footloose industries also share a characteristic in that technical constraints, such as those already discussed, do not impinge on decisions affecting their plant sizes. Both groups of industries are free to organise on either a large scale or a small scale. The fact that there is a strong tendency for large plants to prevail substantiates the point made in Chapter 1 that high localisation of industry is primarily due to the opportunities it affords for the realisation of internal economies of scale.

It is interesting to compare the Irish experience of plant size and localisation inter-action with that which emerges from a study of the two variables in Britain. Florence found that prevalent plant size tended to increase with the degree of localisation up to a point but among the most highly localised industries there was a predominance of medium sized plants. (1) There is certainly no tendency for this latter phenomenon to be duplicated in Ireland. On the contrary, highly localised industries have a strong, large plant orientation—15 of the 17 large plant industries have C.O.L.'s greater than 0·50 while large plant industries account for almost three-quarters of the industries with C.O.L.'s greater than 0·50. What then are the causes of this basic difference in trends? As far as the British pattern is concerned, Florence attributed the association of medium plants with high localisation to the economies of juxtaposition or agglomeration. It was held that a localisation of many medium or even small plants conferred the same economies as a single large plant employing the same total of workers. In other words, localisation economies, particularly those connected with specialisation, have played a major role in determining plant size structures in Britain. In contrast, these economies were largely ruled out as factors influencing localisation among Irish industries. It is time then to look at the question of specialisation a little more carefully, and in particular its relationship to plant size.

3.3 The economic consequences of specialisation

It is helpful to distinguish between two types of specialisation. Product-mix specialisation occurs when production is standardised to a single variety or a few varieties of a specific product or when only a narrow range of products is produced. Process specialisation occurs when firms carry out one or a few processes on their material inputs.

Vertical disintegration provides the mainspring for the growth of specialisation. When demand has reached a certain level firms find it economically attractive to concentrate on a narrower range of products or processes. Many of the activities they carried out are now siphoned off to other firms so that it is not unusual for 'master' firms to develop which are serviced by a complex of small specialised firms. In highly sophisticated economies the most important forms of specialisation occur in the capital goods industries. Capital-saving innovations come about if productivity in these industries is improved, or if the productive capacity of the equipment produced is raised, or both. The degree to which such innovations are realised depends to a large extent on the opportunities for specialisation and division of labour in the capital goods sector. When demand is sufficiently high, vertical disintegration will create dynamic external economies for many other industries as a result of the cost reductions in capital goods. Since some firms will now be concentrating on narrower ranges of capital production, there will be an increasing impetus to develop more specialised capital equipment. If these efforts are successful many of the indivisibilities in certain forms of existing equipment will be reduced or overcome. Hence, for all firms using such equipment minimum economic size will be reduced.

Though the impact of vertical disintegration in other sectors may be less dramatic it does, nevertheless, stimulate the growth of small firms and the entry of new ones. It permits firms to reach more easily the minimum economic size necessary for maximum technical efficiency. Because of the development of many specialist agencies and services new firms need not undertake these operations themselves while older firms may discard them. Thus, firms can start at a higher level of specialisation and hence of efficiency.

However, there is one powerful deterrent to the progressive expansion of specialisation, namely, the level of demand. The literature on this topic reiterates Adam Smith's famous dictum that 'the division of labour is limited by the extent of the market'. Nowhere is this more true than in the case of the capital goods industries. The level of demand necessary to induce the development of the most basic of these industries is beyond the scope of all but the most developed economies while the growth required for the type of specialisation discussed is even more difficult to attain. Indeed, it has been found that in Britain market size is not yet sufficiently developed to permit the specialisation of a number of industries. (28)

The fact then that Ireland is beset by the limits of small market size is hardly cause for surprise. An apt expression of its effects is found in the C.I.O. synthesis of survey team reports which notes that 'much production has been undertaken on a smaller scale than the optimum and the policy of protection has encouraged firms to provide as great a proportion of home demand as possible. This has resulted in a low degree of specialisation and great diverisification'. (14)

Can anything be said then about the relationship between plant size, localisation and the degree of specialisation? Consider the relative importance in terms of net output and employment of the various industries in each localisation grouping. (Table 3.3) At first it might appear that industries

TABLE 3·3

Size of Industries in Location groups: transportable goods industries

Localisation	% net output	% employment	industry size net output	industry size employment	size index net output	size index employment
0·0–0·19	10·67	12·55	5·34	6·27	100	100
0·20–0·29	10·31	10·77	3·44	3·59	64	57
0·30–0·39	7·02	5·09	2·34	1·70	44	27
0·40–0·44	8·17	9·13	1·63	1·83	31	29
0·45–0·49	20·53	24·67	2·93	3·52	55	56
0·39–0·49	28·70	33·80	2·39	2·82	45	45
0·50–0·59	26·32[a]	21·35	2·02[b]	1·64	38	26
0·60–over	13·78	13·65	1·25	1·24	23	20
0·0–0·44	36·17	37·54	2·78	2·89	142	151
0·45–over	60·63	59·67	1·96	1·92	100	100
0·0–0·49	56·70	62·21	2·84	3·11	170	213
0·50–over	40·10	35·00	1·67	1·46	100	100

(a) excluding brewing: 18·70   (b) excluding brewing: average size = 1·56

with low and moderate localisation (0–0·49) assume a dominant position since they account for 57 per cent of net output and 62 per cent of employment. But this is misleading, since the 'balance of power', is held by industries moderately localised (0·45–0·49). If these industries are regrouped with those highly localised the opposite result occurs, namely industries of moderate and high localisation become the most important. Now look at the average size of industries in each category. Average size can be ascertained by dividing the proportion of net output and employment in each group by the number of industries in that category. (Table 3.3) Here there is no doubt. On the basis of either criterion those industries which are highly localised are the smallest industries. They are less than half the size of other industries on the employment criterion and less than threequarters their size in terms of net output. It seems then, that the highly localised industries are significantly different from other industries in at least two important and rather anomalous respects: they tend to be smaller than other industries and at the same time they tend to have relatively larger plant structures.

It may be argued that the smaller average size of the highly localised industries is due to their relatively high level of specialisation *vis-à-vis* other industries. It will be recalled that the process of vertical disintegration requires a breaking up of one industry into a number of smaller sub-industries. Thus, other things being equal, a small industry should tend to specialise in a narrower range of products than other industries. This hypothesis can be tested by calculating an index of the product range for industries in each localisation category. This is done by dividing the number of product classes enumerated by the census for the industries in each group by the number of industries concerned. Table 3.4 shows quite clearly that the

TABLE 3·4

Average product range of industries in different localisation groupings

0–0·19	0·20–0·29	0·30–0·39	0·40–0·49	0·50–0·59	0·60 & over	0·0–0·49	0·50 & over
15	13	12	12	9	7	12	8

level of specialisation when measured in this way is much higher among the highly localised industries. However, it cannot be over-emphasised that this conclusion, based on a single and none-too-impressive measure of specialisation, is extremely tentative.

Indeed, the use of census data to derive measures of specialisation is open to many objections. Besides the problems mentioned in Chapter 1 of defining an industry, C.I.P. data suffer from two other major drawbacks. The first relates to the extent of industry coverage. While the census enumerates the principal product classes manufactured in each industry it gives no breakdown of number of varieties within each class. Thus a measure of product—mix specialisation referring to product classes rather than to a single product has little or no interpretative value. The second problem concerns vertical disintegration. There is likely to be a considerable time-lag between the vertical disintegration of an industry and the disaggregation of census data for its constituent activities on a separate industry basis. In Ireland this lag is aggravated by the small absolute size of industry and the necessity to conceal the identity of particular firms. Thus at any time aggregate data for an industry, as defined by the census, may understate the level of specialisation. One final point must be stressed. Industry specialisation in the strict meaning of the sense is practically non-existent in Ireland. It would be much more precise, therefore, to talk of a relatively low degree of diversification among highly localised industries than to imply that they are specialised in any real and significant way.

3.4 Conclusion

It was found that there is a direct relationship between the level of localisation in an industry and its prevalent size of plant. Industries with low localisation have small plants, and as localisation increases plant sizes tend to become larger. Since low localisation industries are either residentiary or supply-oriented it appears that their plant sizes are primarily determined by technological constraints arising out of the nature of the activity they carry out. In the case of more highly localised industries these conditions are not present so that plant size is free to vary. The fact that large plants tend to predominate among highly localised industries suggests that in the past the opportunities to exploit internal economies of scale have been the major influence of plant size decisions.

British industries, on the other hand, are characterised by a somewhat different structure. Although plant size tends to increase with the level of localisation, highly localised industries have a marked tendency to have medium plants. Florence ascribes this pattern to localisation economies and in particular to the economies of specialisation. In other words, vertical disintegration accompanied by increasing levels of specialisation creates external economies which in time modify the plant size structure most advantageous for an industry. But this process will only occur if the level of demand is sufficiently high and if it grows at a sustained rate. Thus, in Ireland, and indeed in any other developing economy, these conditions have impeded the growth of specialisation.

This raises the question of the weight that can be attached to inter-country comparisions of plant sizes. Besides the shortcomings of unweighted averages, etc. mentioned in Chapter 2, a more fundamental objection now appears. The plant size structure of an industry is related to the stage of development of the industry itself, interdependent industries and the over-all level of activity in the economy. The fact, then, that plant sizes in the same industry in two countries may be classified as small may not reflect a basic similarity in the structure of the industry in both countries but rather may underline the divergence between their developmental stages. Small plants in one country may be due to smallness of markets while in the other small plants may indicate specialisation. The same applies if an industry's plants tend to be large in one country and medium or small in another. The bold statement that the size structure of the industry in one country tends to be larger than in the other conveys no useful information. Indeed, considering the tendency to equate largeness with efficiency, and smallness with inefficiency, the emotive implications of such a statement may be downright misleading. Thus, inter-country comparisons of plant sizes have a doubtful value. As a rule they should be avoided, and if they are made should only involve countries at the same stages of development.

4 CONCENTRATION OF IRISH INDUSTRY

4.1 Introduction

In a model economy, with pure competition, the price system accurately reflects supply and demand and is the means of allocating resources in the most efficient way. But competition is rarely pure and the existence of monopoly, oligopoly or protection from foreign competition by trade barriers affects the movement of prices so that they are no longer the result of impersonal forces.

The domination of an industry by a few producers increases opportunities for price-fixing, collusion and restrictive practices. Prices then no longer reflect marginal costs and marginal products and therefore no longer reflect consumer preferences. Where entrance to an industry is difficult for new firms—because, for example, the level of capital investment required is prohibitive—existing firms may become wasteful and inefficient through lack of competition. Other things being equal, an industry characterised by high concentration is likely to be less competitive than a low concentration industry. However, an element of competitive oligopoly may favour economic growth by encouraging innovation, one of the great spurs to economic development. (58) In Western economies the research which leads to innovation is carried out mainly by large firms which can afford to invest in lengthy research projects. Thus high concentration by itself does not necessarily indicate inefficiency.

In this chapter, four aspects of concentration are examined. First, some problems of measurement are reviewed. Then concentration levels in Irish industry are analysed. A basis for classifying industries according to prevalent market structures is set out. And finally, relationships are sought between levels of concentration and other industry characteristics.

4.2 Measures of concentration

The primary purpose of a concentration ratio is to provide a reliable estimate of the degree to which a few firms may control a particular market i.e. the degree of monopoly power. These ratios may be designed for either an industry or a product class. Ratios will be affected at the industry level by the range of products within the industry and on a product group basis by the classification of products within the group. Where products can be substituted for one another exclusive production of a particular product does not necessarily imply monopoly. So a measure of concentration in terms of a product group should cover all products which may be regarded as substitutes for one another.

The market must be defined: to take market size as being synonymous with domestic industry size is misleading since a proportion of the industry's output may be exported and a proportion of demand for the product may be met by imports.

Since Ireland is heavily dependent on foreign trade, and since much of her industry was established behind tariff barriers, measures of industrial concentration which are confined to a consideration of the extent to which a firm dominates the domestic market are obviously inadequate as indexes of competitiveness in the broad sense. It should, therefore, be borne in mind that the attempt to measure concentration and competitiveness presented in the present chapter needs to be supplemented with additional empirical data on the extent of effective protection and the degree of export orientation in each industry and perhaps also comparative data on the time pattern of prices and productivity in the Irish industry compared with its counterparts in other European countries.

Among the most commonly used measures of industry size are gross output, net output and employment. Of these, gross output is probably the least effective measure since it permits possibilities of double-counting in the case of firms which manufacture part of their own input requirements or provide themselves with ancillary services. If such vertically integrated concerns are among the largest, the concentration ratio will overstate the degree of concentration for the finished products. While a net output indicator remedies this defect, it is liable to

error because of incorrect compilations of inter-plant trans-
actions. Employment as a yardstick of size tends to understate
the level of concentration since larger firms tend to be more
capital intensive than smaller ones.

The enumerative approach provides the simplest, most
widely used, and probably most suitable measure of industry
concentration. An index of concentration is derived by calculating the proportion of total industry size accounted for by a
selected number (usually three or four) of the largest firms or
plants. However, the use of concentration ratios as indicators
of the degree of monopoly needs to be qualified by other data.
The number of units in an industry is important since, regardless of the concentration ratio, the possibilities of oligopolistic
behaviour etc. are greater the smaller the number of units in an
industry. Another significant factor is the size ratio of an
industry. A size ratio expresses the disparity between the
largest units in an industry and all other units. It is derived by
dividing the average size of the selected largest units (in terms
of net output, employment, etc.) by the average size of all other
units in the industry. Again, regardless of the level of concentration, a large size ratio gives some indication of the extent to
which large firms may dominate an industry. An increase in
size ratios over time increases the scope for the domination of
smaller firms and may lead to a decline in competition.

4.3 Concentration levels in Irish industry

In Ireland, the law prohibits the C.S.O. from presenting
C.I.P. data in any way which might reveal the identity of
individual firms. This ruled out the possibility of deriving concentration ratios based on the performance of the largest firms,
and meant that indices of concentration accounting for the
performance of the largest plants had to be used instead.
However, firm concentration in an industry cannot be lower
than plant concentration since each firm must operate at least
one plant. Thus, a plant concentration measure represents the
minimum degree of concentration in an industry. It is also
unlikely that there would be much difference between a firm
concentration ratio, and a plant concentration ratio for any

industry, since the industrial structure is essentially of a single plant character. (25)

The ratios were designed for industries as defined and classified by the C.I.P. This approach, of course, is not entirely satisfactory because of the wide range of products manufactured in some industries and the fact that some of these products cannot be regarded as substitutes for each other. The problem of lack of substitutability is most prevalent in the metal trades (cutlery and manufacture of wire); paper and paper products (cardboard boxes, etc. and stationery); chemicals and drugs (cattle dips and toilet powder); electrical machinery and appliances (T.V. sets and neon signs). It also occurs to a lesser extent in the wood and cork industry, fellmongery and jute and canvas. In these industries, therefore, the degree of sub-industry concentration is likely to be understated.

Three measures of concentration were calculated: (i) the proportion of employment accounted for by the four plants which were largest in terms of employment, (ii) the proportion of net output accounted for by the same four plants, and (iii), the proportion of net output accounted for by the four plants largest in terms of net output.

From one point of view it would make no difference which of these measures were used to study concentration since industries designated as having high, medium or low concentration on the basis of one criterion are also ranked similarly by the other two. The choice of measure, therefore, only affects the relative position of industries within the specific concentration classes. However, notwithstanding the similarity of rankings, there are a number of points which suggest that size is best measured in terms of net output, and accordingly that the third measure should be selected. For one thing, a comparison of measures (i) and (ii) reveals that in 21 of the 48 industries analysed, the four plants largest in terms of employment accounted for a higher proportion of industry net output than of industry employment. In other words, in almost half of the industries the plants largest in terms of employment are larger still in terms of net output. This is most noticeable in the case of such food industries as butter blending and margarine, bread and flour confectionery, soft drinks, cocoa, chocolate and sugar confectionery, the printing and publishing trades, the fertiliser industry, and structural clay products. Secondly, a comparison of measures (*i*) and (*iii*) shows that in only twenty industries are the plants which are largest in terms of employment also largest in terms of net output. These observations support the thesis that an employment criterion of concentration tends to understate the size of large firms or plants since it fails to take account of their relatively higher capital intensity. For this reason, therefore, measure (*iii*) is used in the current study.

4.4 Levels of industry concentration in 1964

No established criteria exist for the categorisation of industries into high, medium and low concentration so it was thought best to follow the classification system devised by Eveley and Little in their major study of concentration in British industry. (29) Consequently, a high concentration industry is defined as one in which the four largest plants account for at least 67 per cent of industry net output; a medium concentration industry is one in which the four largest plants account for between 34 per cent and 66 per cent of net output while industries in which the four largest plants account for less than 34 per cent of net output are regarded as low concentration industries.

Consider first the high concentration industries. Reference to Table 4.1 shows that 15 industries fall into this category, and that they account for 23 per cent of manufacturing industry net output, and for 17 per cent of employment. It will be noticed also that the number of units in these industries is small. Seven have less than ten units while only one has more than 30, the average for the group being 13. The group contains almost one-third of the food industries, and these in turn account for almost one-third of high concentration industries.

In general, the type of activity carried out varies a great deal as between members of the group. It ranges from the manufacture of final demand goods to intermediate goods (cement, railroad equipment, etc.) and includes both assembly and continuing processing trades.

Twenty-two industries (Table 4.2) have ratios indicating medium concentration. This group is by far the largest, account-

TABLE 4·1

High concentration industries in 1964

Industry	ind. net output as % of net output of all man. industry	ind. em. as % of em. of all man. industry	no of units
Butter blending	0·41	0·18	10
Distilling	0·55	0·41	9
Cocoa & chocolate	2·40	3·03	38
Brewing	7·01	2.83	8
Sugar	1·34	1·44	4
Cement*	1·59	0·68	2
Glass & pottery	1·66	1·71	25
Fertilisers	1·71	0·94	25
Soaps & detergents	0·45	0·43	9
Ships & boats	0·74	0·72	11
Assembly of other vehicles	0·77	0·81	13
Fellmongery	1·06	0·98	23
Tobacco	2·56	1·32	8
Railroad equipment	0·92	1·41	1
Brushes & brooms*	0·18	0·25	12
Total high concentration industries	23·35	17·14	198

*estimated

ing for more than two-fifths of manufacturing industry net output and employment. The number of plants varies considerably, the largest recorded being for bread and flour confectionery, and printing and publishing. Indeed, the number of units in these two industries tends to distort the overall average for the group. When both are excluded, the average number of establishments per industry falls from 58 to 44.

The remaining eleven industries (Table 4.3) are characterised by low concentration. It is interesting to observe that while they account for approximately the same proportion of manufacturing industry net output as the high concentration industries they account for almost twice the proportion of

5

TABLE 4·2

Medium concentration industries in 1964

Industry	ind. net output as % of net output of all man. industry	ind. em. as % of em. of all man. industry	no of units
Malting	0·47	0·41	32
Canning of fruit	1·57	2·05	29
Soft drinks	1·16	0·94	80
Bread, biscuits & flour confectionery	4·72	5·52	333
Beef, mutton etc.	1·90	1·37	37
Flour milling	1·47	1·35	26
Miscellaneous food & canning of fish (2)	0·41	0·54	31
Shirtmaking	0·69	1·40	30
Boots & shoes	2·94	3.62	39
Printing & publishing	5.76	5·61	172
Paper & paper products	2.98	3·00	52
Structural clay products	1.20	1.20	94
Oils & paints	1.28	0·83	37
Made-up textiles	0·28	0·45	13
Hosiery	2.91	3·87	64
Linen & cotton	1·94	2·32	30
Jute & canvas	1·88	2·31	45
Assembly of mechanical vehicles	4·28	3·68	63
Electrical machinery	3·71	4·24	70
Machinery except electrical	1·55	1·54	63
Leather goods	0·31	0·48	26
Total medium concentration industries	43·41	46·73	1,366

employment. There is also a clear-cut difference between this group and the other two in the matter of plant numbers. The overall average number of plants per industry for the group is 115, which is nine times as high as the average for the high concentration group, and twice as high as the average for the medium concentration industries.

It may be asked whether some groups of industries are more prone to high concentration than others. In Table 4.4 industries have been aggregated on the basis of the group classifi-

TABLE 4·3

Low concentration industries in 1964

Industry	ind. net output as % of net output of all man. industry	ind. em. as % of em. of all man. industry	no of units
Dairy products	3·06	2·91	219
Bacon	2·52	2·54	39
Animal feeds	1·35	1·70	151
Clothing (men's & boys') Clothing (miscellaneous) Clothing (women's & girls')	4·54	8·16	281
Wood & cork	1·68	2·06	154
Furniture*	1·52	2·19	145
Chemicals & drugs	1·54	1·23	67
Woollen & worsted	3·01	4·04	47
Metal trades	6·03	6·24	177
Total low concentration industries	25·25	31·07	1,280

*estimated.

TABLE 4·4

Concentration in industry groups 1964

	employment criterion			net output criterion		
	concentration ratio	plant size ratio	net output control	concentration ratio	plant size ratio	no of units
Food industry	48·3	14·1	61·9	63·4	26·2	1,064
Clothing & footwear	26·2	5·1	30·9	31·5	6·6	350
Textiles	42·0	6·5	43·1	44·3	7·1	199
Wood & furniture	21·4	6·8	23·0	27·1	9·2	311
Printing & publishing	34·6	12·6	40·7	43·2	23·9	224
Chemicals	50·5	24·8	55·1	57·7	8·0	138
Glass, cement & structural clay products	63·3	19·1	73·2	73·7	31·1	121
Metal & engineering	46·5	12·4	48·7	49·0	13·8	398
Miscellaneous	79·9	14·9	71·6	71·9	9·6	57

cation system used in the C.I.P. However, the resultant ratios do not reflect levels of concentration in the strict meaning of the word since the products of the trades aggregated are not, in most cases, substitutes for each other. It is better, therefore, to look upon the ratios as giving some indication of the extent to which the four largest plants in each of the industries within a group dominate the group as a whole. Bearing this in mind, it seems that high concentration is most prevalent among the industries in the two groups comprised of food products, and glass, cement and structural clay products. In addition to high concentration ratios both groups also reveal large plant-size ratios suggesting considerable leeway for the exercise of monopoly power by the largest plants in some or all of the constituent industries. On the other hand, large plants would appear to have least control in the clothing and footwear group and the wood and furniture industries since both groups have not only relatively low concentration ratios but also smaller-than-average plant size ratios.

4.5 Prevalent market structures

This question of the control the largest plants in an industry may exercise can be examined in more detail by analysing concentration levels in conjunction with plant size ratios, prevalent plant size structures and the number of units in each industry.

A substantial degree of monopoly is likely in those industries which have high concentration and a small number of units. From Table 4.5 it is apparent that 14 industries fit this description. In all they account for approximately 21 per cent of net output and 14 per cent of employment. The number of units in each of these industries is small being less than 13 in all but three cases. Even then, while the three industries concerned have each more than 20 units, their concentration ratios are extremely high. It seems then that about one-fifth of Irish manufacturing industry output is subject to a high degree of monopoly control.

At the other end of the scale are the industries which most closely conform to the stipulations of pure competition (Table 4.6). They may be divided into three groups, each succeeding one being one step further away from the purely competitive ideal. First, there are seven industries characterised by a low concentration ratio, a below average plant size ratio (less than 15), a small plant size structure and many establishments. The second group comprises two industries each of which has a low concentration ratio, a below average plant size ratio, and many units. And finally, it may be said, but with less certainty, that monopoly elements are also likely to be of little consequence in the ten industries which have medium concentration ratios, below average plant size ratios and many establishments.

In the 15 remaining industries (Table 4.7), accounting for

TABLE 4·5

Industries with monopoly characteristics

Industry	net output as % of man. ind. net output	employment as % of man. ind. em.
Butter blending	0·41	0·18
Distilling	0·55	0·41
Brewing	7·01	2·83
Sugar	1·34	1·44
Glass & pottery	1·66	1·71
Cement*	1·59	0·68
Fertilisers	1·71	0·94
Soaps & detergents	0·45	0·43
Ships & boats	0·74	0·72
Assembly of other vehicles	0·77	0·81
Fellmongery	1·06	0·98
Tobacco	2.56	1·32
Railroad equipment	0·92	1·41
Brushes & brooms*	0·18	0.25
Total	20·95	14·11

*estimated
NOTE: Sugar, cement & railroad equipment have concentration ratios of 100%. They may be regarded as having size ratios of less than 5·0 since the average size of the largest, or the two & three largest plants in each is less than five times the size of other plants.

TABLE 4·6

Industries with characteristics of perfect competition

Industry	net output as % of man. ind. net output	employment as % of man. ind. em.
(a)		
Dairy products	3·06	2·91
Animal foods	1·35	1·70
Clothing (3)	4·54	8·16
Furniture	1·52	2.19
Chemicals & drugs	1·54	1·23
	12·01	16·19
(b)		
Bacon	2·52	2·54
Woollen & worsted	3·01	4·04
	5·53	6·58
(c)		
Malting	0·47	0·41
Shirtmaking	0·69	1·40
Boots & shoes	2·94	3·62
Paper	2.98	3·00
Oils & paints	1·28	0·83
Hosiery	2·91	3·87
Linen & cotton	1·94	2·32
Jute & canvas	1·88	2·31
Electrical machinery	3·71	4·24
Machinery except electrical	1·55	1·54
	20·35	23·54
TOTAL	37·89	46·31

33 per cent of net output and 35 per cent of employment, some degree of oligopolistic behaviour seems likely to exist either because the number of units is small or because a large plant size ratio indicates the scope for leadership by a few plants.

To summarise, then, it appears that 60 per cent of the industries analysed (29 out of 48), accounting for 54 per cent of manufacturing industry net output and 49 per cent of employment have sufficient characteristics to suggest that they have a strong monopolistic or oligopolistic orientation. Since the

TABLE 4·7

Industries with oligopoly characteristics

Industry	net output as % of man. ind. net output	employment as % of man. ind. em.
Wood & cork	1·68	2·06
Metal trades	6·03	6·24
Canning of fruit	1·57	2·05
Soft drinks	1·16	0·94
Bread & biscuits etc.	4·72	5·52
Beef & mutton etc.	1·90	1·37
Flour milling	1·47	1·35
Misc. foods & canning of fish (2)	0·41	0·54
Printing and publishing	5·76	5·61
Structural clay products*	1·20	1·20
Made-up textiles	0·28	0·45
Assembly of vehicles	4·28	3·68
Leather goods	0·31	0·48
Cocoa and chocolate	2·40	3·03
TOTAL	33·17	34·52

*estimated

measures used reflect the minimum degree of concentration, etc., it must be concluded that oligopolistic competition in one form or another is the most prevalent type in Irish industry.

It should be pointed out, of course, that the mere existence of the scope for monopoly power does not necessarily mean that it will be fully exploited. In most countries there is a considerable body of legislation dealing with the control of monopoly practices. In Ireland, the Restrictive Trade Practice Act of 1953 provides the legal framework for the regulation of competition. Although it maintains that restrictive business practices are not always contrary to the public interest it does prohibit producers from arbitrarily imposing such restrictions even when the warranted special conditions exist. The Act also provided for the establishment of the Fair Trade Commission. This body may hold public inquiries into arrangements relating to the production and sale of goods and services. The Commission reports its findings to the Minister for Industry and Commerce who may make an order prohibiting a specific practice if he considers it contrary to the public good. Furthermore, as a result of the Prices Act 1958, the Minister is empowered to set ceiling prices for commodities if their excessive prices are regarded as being the result of monopoly practices. A second reason producers may be reluctant to exercise their monopoly power is concerned with profit maximisation. Although a monopoly price may result in large profits in the short run, it may also invite government intervention, or encourage rival producers attracted by the prospects of high profit to enter the industry. Even when the costs of entry are high, a producer may be inclined to set a price fairly close to the competitive level since rival producers may be less willing to incur the high cost of entry if their profits will be only slightly above the normal level.

Returning to Tables 4.5, 4.6, and 4.7, it may be noted, in conclusion, that the data bear out the findings of the preceding section regarding the concentration of industry groups. Of the 16 industries in the food group, only four have the characteristics of pure competition, while each of the industries in the glass, cement and structural clay products group is either monopoly or oligopoly oriented, the bias being strongly in favour of monopoly. And although the wood and cork industry has an oligopolistic market structure, the clothing and furniture trades are among the most competitive industries.

4.6 Concentration and other economic variables

The following section will analyse the relations between levels of concentration and other variables: industry size, level of investment, prevalent plant size structure, plant size ratios and localisation. Since it is unlikely that concentration is the result of random forces distinct patterns may be expected to emerge.

Consider first the relation between size of industry and level of concentration. The average industry size in each concentration group can be calculated by dividing the proportions of manufacturing industry net output and employment accounted for by each group by the number of industries in the group. It is clear from Table 4.8 that the high concentration

TABLE 4·8

Levels of concentration & industry size

Concentration	% of employment	% of net output	employment index	net output index
High	1·143	1·596	100	100
Medium	2·070	1·919	181	120
Low	2·824	2·296	247	144

industries are the smallest by either criterion and low concentration industries the largest. In other words, the association indicates that the smaller the size of an industry the higher the level of concentration. This result is not, of course, unexpected, for the smaller an industry the more specialised it tends to be and the smaller its product mix. And, as already pointed out, concentration ratios tend to be higher the more narrowly defined the group of products.

One way of looking at the barriers to the entry of new plants into an industry is in terms of the minimum economic size of plant which a producer must establish in order to compete efficiently with existing plants. Other things being equal, the larger the minimum size of plant required the more formidable the barrier to entry. Thus it may be hypothesised that industries where large prevalent plant size structures are caused either by economies of scale or technical factors should tend to be highly concentrated, while industries with small plant characteristics should have low concentration. The extent of the relation between the two variables—plant size and concentration—is shown in Tables 4·9 and 4·10, and it bears out the hypothesis. In precise terms, as plant size increases con-

TABLE 4·9

Contingency table of concentration & plant size

No of industries	plant size	no of industries with concentration			% distribution of industries with concentration		
		low	medium	high	low	medium	high
19	Small	7	9	3	36·8	47·4	15·8
6	Medium	1	3	2	16·7	50·0	33·3
25	Small & medium	8	12	5	32·0	48·0	20·0
16	Large	1	5	10	6·3	31·2	62·5

TABLE 4·10

Contingency table of plant size & level of concentration

No of industries	concentration	no of industries with plant sizes				% distribution of industries with plant sizes			
		small	medium	small & medium	large	small	medium	small & medium	large
9	low	7	1	8	1	77·7	11·1	88·8	11·2
17	medium	9	3	12	5	52·9	17·6	70·5	29·5
15	high	3	2	5	10	20·0	13·3	33·3	66·3
41		19	6	25	16				

centration increases, and the converse relation also holds, namely that as concentration increases plant sizes tend to become larger. High concentration industries are predominantly large plant industries while low concentration industries in contrast have generally small plants. In other words, concentration is low in those industries in which plant size is not a barrier to entry.

A few words should be said, however, about those industries which have high concentration ratios and small plant sizes. Three industries are involved—fertilisers, butter blending etc., and brushes and brooms. On the basis of horse-power per head both fertilisers and butter blending etc. are highly capitalised, ranking first and seventh respectively. Thus employment as a criterion of establishment size probably understates real size in terms of labour and capital. This suggests that high concentration is due to the high capital costs of entry since the minimum economic size in terms of capital seems to be large. As regards the brushes and brooms industry, no statistics of horse-power per head are available. However, the C.I.O. survey team report on the industry would suggest that it is at least moderately capitalised and this may have been a factor influencing its concentration. The principal cause of concentration, however, is the small size of market, for the industry accounts for less than 0·2 per cent of total manufacturing industry net output.

A distinction should be made between the prevalent plant size structure of an industry and the minimum economic size required for efficient production—a distinction clarified by use of a plant size ratio. A high plant size ratio means that there is a significant difference between the size of the largest units in an industry and the size of all other units. Now, if the existence of plants in an industry is taken as proof of their ability to compete, then a high plant size ratio also implies that small units may compete effectively even though they are very much at a size disadvantage in relation to the largest units. Thus, the minimum economic size of plant for the industry is small. It will also be small in the case of industries which have both small plant size ratios and small prevalent plant sizes. On the other hand plant size as an obstacle to entry is likely to be most effective in the case of industries in which plant size ratios are small and prevalent plant sizes are large.

The average plant size ratio for all industries is 15. Accordingly, industries with ratios greater than 15 are classified as high size ratio industries while a ratio lower than five indicates a low size ratio industry. Two points emerge from Table 4.11. First, it may be inferred that low concentration

TABLE 4·11

Contingency table of concentration & plant size ratios

No	concentra-tion	no of industries with plant size ratios:				% of industries with plant size ratios:			
		0·0–5·0	5·1–14·9	0·0–14·9	15–over	0·0–5·0	5·1–14·9	0·0–14·9	15–over
11	Low	3	7	10	1	27·3	63·7	91·0	9·0
22	Medium	6	11	17	5	27·3	50·0	77·3	22·7
15	High	4	5	9	6	26·6	33·3	60·0	40·0

industries have low to medium size ratios. Since they are also characterised by small plant sizes it is reasonable to conclude that plant size is not a barrier to entry as far as these industries are concerned. It would be untrue to say, however, that high concentration industries have high size ratios. It may only be observed that they have a higher proportion of high size ratio industries than either the medium or low concentration groups. But it is also apparent that more than a quarter of high concentration industries have low size ratios. The industries concerned—cement, sugar, railroad equipment and tobacco—are typified by large plant sizes while the number of units in each is extremely small. In these industries, therefore, minimum economic plant size tends to be large so that plant size appears to be a serious obstacle to entry. It comes as no surprise, then,

that two of the industries—sugar and railroad equipment—
are, in fact, state-run monopolies.

There are six industries with high plant size ratios and
medium or low concentration. Of these, three are residentiary
(bread and flour, soft drinks, and wood and cork); two are
supply-oriented (structural clay products, and assembly of
motor vehicles); and one—printing and publishing—is market-
oriented. In addition, each industry has a small plant size
structure except for printing and publishing for which no
prevalent plant size could be computed. In the case of the
residentiary and supply-oriented industries plant sizes, it will
be recalled, are determined by the relative densities of supplies
and markets. High plant size ratios indicate, therefore, significantly larger scales of production in regions with markets
or supplies of the highest density. As regards the residentiary
industries it may be surmised that increasing market concentration will lead to increasing industry plant concentration.
Indeed, the data suggest that this interaction has in fact
occurred between 1954 and 1964 in those industries whose
markets are the general population. (3)

What is the overall nature of the relation between concentration and localisation? Data for those industries for which
both a C.O.L. and a concentration ratio could be computed
is set out in contingency chart form in Table 4.12. It is apparent

TABLE 4·12

Contingency table of localisation & concentration

No of industries	local-isation	no of industries with concentration				percentage of industries with concentration			
		low	medium	low & medium	high	low	medium	low & medium	high
4	0·0–0·29	2	2	4	—	50·0	50·0	100	—
3	0·30–0·39	1	2	3	—	33·3	66·7	100	—
11	0·40–0·49	4	6	10	1	36·4	54·5	90·9	9·1
13	0·50–0·59	1	7	8	5	7·7	53·9	61·6	38·4
11*	0·60–over	—	4	4	7	—	36·0	36·0	63·9

*Cement is highly localised

that as localisation increases concentration tends to become higher. The highly localised industries are in general high concentration industries. The relation may also be stated in converse form: high concentration industries tend to be highly localised (12 out of the 14 high concentration industries involved have C.O.L.'s greater than 0·50) while industries with low concentration tend to be dispersed (5 out of the 8 industries concerned have C.O.L.'s lower than 0·44). In other words, plant concentration tends to be low among industries which are tied to dispersed markets or rooted to dispersed sources of material supplies. This means that high enterprise concentration may only occur through the operation of multi-plant firms. However, since the largest plants in these industries usually account for only a small proportion of industry output, etc., enterprise concentration is likely to be low unless one or a few enterprises control the largest plants. Thus it may be expected that industries with low plant concentration and small or medium plant size ratios will have low enterprise concentration. On the other hand, high concentration at both plant and enterprise level is most likely among those industries which are either rooted to specific or few sources of material supplies, or which are 'footloose' with respect to location, and capable of achieving significant internal economies of scale through large scale production. In these industries high localisation may result from the large scale production of a few units in a specific location.

Finally, there remains the question of the relationship between the level of capitalisation of an industry and the level of concentration. Barriers to the entry of new plants may arise for two reasons in industries in which economies of scale are significant or minimum economic size is large. First, a large proportion of industry output may be required for efficient operation. And second, large absolute amounts of capital may be required to achieve the necessary scale of operation. Thus, capital requirements may be so large that entrants can secure the necessary finance either not at all or at rates which would put them at a serious cost disadvantage *vis-à-vis* established plants. Furthermore, small absolute product and capital markets, as in Ireland, put severe restrictions on the number of units which can operate efficiently on a large scale. Consequently, industries with relatively high levels of capital intensity should show relatively higher concentration than other industries. And the converse should also hold, namely, that high concentration industries should tend to be more capital intensive than other industries.

In order to illustrate the relation, recourse was had to an index of horsepower per operative as a measure of capital intensity. More accurately, this index reflects the level of mechanisation in an industry. But even in this sense it may be seriously defective since much mechanisation does not necessarily involve a heavy expenditure on power.[1] Turning to Table 4.13 and

TABLE 4·13

Contingency table of investment & concentration levels

No	hp per head	no distribution				% distribution			
		low	*medium*	*l+m*	*high*	*low*	*medium*	*l+m*	*high*
13	0–1·50	4	8	12	1	30·6	61·5	92·1	7·9
12	1·51–3·00	2	6	8	4	16·6	50·0	66·7	33·3
11	3·10–6·00	3	4	7	4	27·3	36·3	63·6	36·3
10	6·10–over	2	3	5	5	20·0	30·0	50·0	50·0
25	0–3·10	6	14	20	5	24·0	56·0	80·0	20·0
21	3·10–over	5	7	12	9	23·8	33·8	57·6	42·8

reading from top left to bottom right it is clear that there is a definite relationship between concentration and capital intensity. As a result, increasing levels of capital intensity tend to be associated with increasing levels of concentration. But while the proportion of industries with high concentration increases as the level of capital intensity increases, it may not be inferred that capital intensive industries tend to be high concentration industries since only 43 per cent of the industries

[1] Cf. O'Malley (3) Chapter 4, for a description of these problems.

with a horsepower index greater than 3·00 fall into this category. There is, however, a more pronounced tendency for high concentration industries to be associated with high capital intensity, as may be seen in Table 4.14. Almost two-thirds of

TABLE 4·14

Contingency table of concentration & investment levels

No	*concentration*	*no distribution of industries with specified horse power index*					
		0–1·5	1·51–3·0	3·1–6·0	6·1 & over	0–3·0	3·1 & over
11	Low	4	2	3	2	6	5
21	Medium	8	6	4	3	14	7
14	High	1	4	4	5	5	9

		% distribution of industries with specified horse power index					
11	Low	36·3	18·2	27·3	18·2	54·5	45·5
21	Medium	38·1	28·6	19·0	14·3	66·7	33·3
14	High	27·1	28·6	28·6	35·7	35·7	64·3

the high concentration industries have a horsepower index greater than 3·00 while only 36 per cent of the industries in the other concentration groups have a horsepower ranking of similar magnitude. Thus, it seems that among Irish industries in general the level of capital requirements has influenced the level of concentration.

4.7 Conclusion

In this chapter some of the more important aspects of industry concentration were examined. It was found that on the whole Irish industry had a strong oligopolistic tendency. Moreover, such traditionally cited factors as plant size and level of investment appear to play a significant role in determining market structures. As far as concentration is concerned, the Irish experience is normal, at least in the sense that the industrial structures of most developed economies invariably exhibit a marked oligopolistic orientation. But the comparison should not be unduly pressed. In more sophisticated economies high concentration is associated, more often than not, with absolute largeness. That is to say that giant multi-purpose corporate entities dwarf all other enterprises in an industry because of the vast resources at their disposal, invest-ment intensities that run, perhaps, at many times the level of GNP in Ireland and technological bases which are geared to highly-expensive and time-consuming research and develop-ment. Even though such corporations may not explicitly indulge in monopolistic practices in the strict interpretation of the term, the existence of latent seller power is enhanced as a result of their ability to mould consumer preference through the use of such sophisticated weaponry as planned obsolescence, market research, and extensive advertising.

In contrast, concentration among Irish industries can be related, like so many other economic variables, to the small size of markets. It is not a case, therefore, of a few very large concerns each exercising far-reaching market power, for, even at the firm level, the largest in Ireland bears no comparison in size to the national and international corporations of other countries whose monopoly power is so readily identifiable. Rather, it is a question of small numbers of units in most industries so that it is not too difficult for the largest among them to account for a significant proportion of total activity. Whether or not this has led to monopoly exploitation will be further analysed in Chapter 7.

5 INTER-INDUSTRY PRODUCTIVITY ANALYSIS

5.1 Introduction

The technical statistical and conceptual problems attendant on the measurement of industrial productivity are discussed in depth in a number of readily available sources and need not detain us at any length.[1] Only the immediately relevant issues are touched upon briefly in the present discussion.

5.2 Measures of productivity

The term 'productivity' is generally used in reference to the productivity of human labour. Although labour productivity is inadequate as a measure of productivity most economists use it because it does not involve the complex statistical, methodological and conceptual problems associated with more comprehensive measures. In addition, man occupies a unique position in the production structure being both 'the end and the agent of production'. From a social viewpoint, therefore, 'current human labour should be rendered scarce in comparison to other inputs and to output. The goal should be a simultaneous and steady increase in real output and voluntary leisure, i.e. economic welfare'. (30)

In Ireland, gross volume indexes of production are computed for 47 industries and published annually in the Census of Industrial Production. A Fisher-type formula on a chain basis is used to adjust the value of gross output for price changes. The correlative quantity and value data collected at the census for the current year and similar data for the previous year are used to derive two price indexes. One is weighted with current year quantities and the other is weighted with previous year quantities while the previous year is taken as base year. The geometric mean of these indexes is taken as the final price

[1]Cf. McGilvray, *Irish Economic Statistics* (55) Chapter 4.

72

index of an industry's products. The gross output value index divided by the price index gives a volume index for the industry, as between consecutive years. This index is then linked to the base year which is 1953.

An index of gross labour productivity is derived by dividing an index of gross production for a producing unit (a single firm, an industry, a sector or the whole economy) by an index of labour usage (man-hours or employees). For example, one form of the index is

$$\frac{\Sigma Q_{1i} P_{0i}}{\Sigma Q_{0i} P_{0i}} \left| \frac{N_1}{N_0} \times 100 \right.$$

where P and Q refer to price and quantity respectively, N_0 is the total employment in the industry in year 0 and N_1 employment in year 1.

In general, gross labour productivity measures should be supplemented by other measures designed to provide comparisons of the use of raw materials and fuel per unit of output, and if at all possible data on the labour required to maintain capital equipment. For it may very well happen that economies in the use of labour are purchased at the expense of diseconomies in the use of other resources so that a higher labour productivity is counterbalanced by the lower productivity of other resources. For example, if capital is substituted for labour the resultant rise in labour productivity may be accompanied by a fall in the productivity of capital.

An index of gross labour productivity may also be misleading as a measure of productivity movements over time. As an industry grows there is a tendency for vertical disintegration to occur. In other words, the industry carries out fewer fabrication processes, there is a corresponding fall in the ratio of net output to gross output and a fall in labour requirements per unit of gross output. While part of this reduction in unit labour requirements may represent a reduction in real costs, part also reflects the fall in the ratio of net output to gross output. Hence the resultant increase in productivity associated with the movement of gross output and labour would be considerably larger than the increase associated with movements in net output and labour.

But despite their limitations, gross labour productivity measures have many uses particularly in times when labour rather than capital imposes a capacity constraint. Here they are most pertinent to the problem of how labour should be allocated. In addition, it seems that gross measures rank industries correctly with respect to real changes in productivity. Indeed, one study found a correlation coefficient as high as 0·91 between movements in labour productivity and total factor productivity which strongly suggests that gross measures are good indicators of real progress. (31)

An index of net productivity of labour avoids many of the deficiencies of gross measures. Besides employing an inherently more valid concept of output, it avoids the difficulties associated with vertical disintegration. The one weak point of the index is the sensitivity of the volume net output component to the interaction of two price indexes (one for gross output, and one for material inputs) which may lead to arithmetic instability especially if both indexes are moving in opposite directions. Significant distortions are most likely to arise the lower the ratio of net output to gross output (32), and the more volatile the relative shifts in both output and input mixes and prices. Indeed, in many cases one of these factors may lead to a negative or very low volume net output—results which are quite meaningless for productivity purposes.

The concept of total factor productivity is an extension of the net productivity of labour. It equates over time volume net output with the real volume of resources used. But, while in theory all inputs should be accounted for, empirically it has been possible to include only labour and capital with occasional allowances for land. Taking the simplest case of a two-factor input model, the index may be written as follows:

$$\frac{\Sigma P_{0i}\,Q_{1i} - \Sigma X_{0j}M_{1j}}{\Sigma P_{0i}\,Q_{0i} - \Sigma X_{0j}M_{0j}} \;\Bigg|\; \frac{W_0 N_1 + R_0 K_1}{W_0 N_0 + R_0 K_0} \times 100$$

where P_{0i} is the unit value (or gross price) of the ith product in year o, M_{0j} is the quantity of the jth material used in the production of the ith product in year o, and X_{0j} is the unit value of the jth material in year o. N_0 and N_1 refer to labour input in physical terms in years o and 1 respectively; K_0 and K_1 to capital input in physical terms, W_0 to the real wage rate in the industry in year o and R_0 to the real return to capital in year o. Since the value of net output in year o must also represent total factor compensation in that year, it follows that

$$\Sigma P_{0i} Q_{0i} = \Sigma X_{0j} M_{0j} + W_0 N_0 + R_0 K_0$$

The total factor productivity index becomes therefore:

$$\frac{\Sigma P_{0i} Q_{1i} - \Sigma X_{0j} M_{1j}}{W_0 N_1 + R_0 K_1} \times 100$$

Some major studies have been carried out using the total factor technique or variants thereof. Productivity is defined as the ratio of arithmetic indexes of output and input.[2] But in designing the index operational assumptions are often made which are incompatible with its conceptual apparatus, and it fails to take account of inputs other than labour and capital. Thus the measure excludes all intangible factors as well as the indirect effects of varying patterns of resource allocation. Indeed, the usual measures of labour and capital provide a clear example of inconsistency in resource treatment. Labour measures, it will be recalled, are based on actual hours worked or total employment and these take no account of the unemployed and the underemployed. Measures of capital, on the other hand relate to capital available regardless of whether it is idle or underutilised.

5.3 Productivity and other economic variables

A number of studies show quite conclusively that significant relationships exist between the behaviour of productivity and other economic variables such as wages, costs, output, and employment. (33, 34) Accordingly, this section will investigate

[2]Total factor productivity may also be expressed in terms of a geometric index. If the production function is written as:

$Y = A^a K^b$, the rate of growth of the geometric index becomes

$$\frac{\bar{A}}{A} = \frac{\bar{Y}}{Y} - \frac{a\bar{L}}{L} - \frac{\bar{K}}{K}$$

where $\bar{A}$, $\bar{Y}$, $\bar{L}$, $\bar{K}$, are $dA/dt/A$, $d/dt/Y$, $dL/dt/L$ and $dK/dt/K$ respectively, and a and b are the weights given to labour and capital inputs.

the extent of similar relations among Irish industries. The variables selected for analysis are similar to those chosen by Salter for his cross-sectional analysis of U.K. and U.S. industries.[3] They include volume of output, employment, output per head (subsequently referred to as productivity) output per operative, earnings per operative, unit labour costs, unit wage costs, unit salary costs, unit material costs, unit gross margin costs, and gross prices.

The volume of output data are production indexes published annually by the Central Statistics Office in the Census of Industrial Production. The employment statistics are averages of the numbers engaged in each industry and are taken from the C.I.P. Output per head corresponds to gross labour productivity and in subsequent discussion it is referred to simply as productivity. Output per operative is a measure of operative productivity. The number of operatives equals employment minus salaried persons. Particulars of the latter are published in the C.I.P. bulletins. Earnings per operative are derived by dividing total wage payments by the number of operatives. Unit labour, material and gross margin costs are the constituent elements of selling price, while unit labour cost may be decomposed into wage and salary costs per unit of output. Unit materials cost includes all raw materials inputs, fuel, packing materials, and in some cases repair and maintainance costs; unit gross margin cost is the residual element in price after deductions have been made for material and labour costs, and has been used in some studies as an indicator of capital costs.(33) It includes depreciation, taxation, rent, interest, profit, and miscellaneous expenses such as advertising, employer contributions to social welfare, and office expenses. And finally, gross output prices have been derived from the formula $V=PQ$ where V is the value index of gross output, Q is the production index and P the desired price index.

It should be realised that the indexes used in the current study are open to all of the usual criticisms. In addition there are three other important sources of error mentioned by Salter.

[3]Since the research underlying the present study was completed, a study of Irish industrial productivity applying similar techniques has been published: Kennedy in *Journal of Statistical and Social Inquiry Society* 1968–69. (56)

First, as noted earlier one cannot talk about the productivity of a single factor. A nexus of interrelated factors is involved. The analysis suffers therefore because such important variables as rates of capital formation, technical change, rates of capital replacement, etc., all of which are closely connected with the movement of productivity, could not be quantified. Second, since all unit cost figures have been derived by using volume output indexes errors in the latter may lead to errors in the other series which may in turn lead to spurious correlations. An upward bias in the output series will cause an upward bias in all indexes in which they are used as numerators and a downward bias where they are denominators. However, after a number of tests, Salter concluded that the element of spuriousness was likely to be small, and there is no compelling reason to believe otherwise, insofar as data in the current study are concerned. Although skewed distributions are a third possible source of error, they do not appear to present a problem since the data in Table 5·1 are largely free from any tendency

TABLE 5·1

Frequency distribution of changes in selected variables 1953–1963

Number of industries	output	employment	output per head	earnings per operative(a)	unit wage cost(a)	unit salary cost(a)	unit labour cost	unit materials cost	unit gross margins cost	gross prices
Over 400	1									
367–399										
334–336						1				
300–333	1							1	1	
267–299	1							1		1
234–266	4	1			1		1		1	
200–233	5	2	2	2	2	2	2		5	
167–199	10	2	5	24	4	7	5	2	6	
134–166	11	11	20	23	13	16	8	4	11	9
100–133	10	21	14		22	21	28	26	19	33
67–99	6	12	9		6	2	6	17	6	7
34–66	1	1			1					
Mean (inc. Elect)	157	113	139	167	121	134	121	104	132	111
Mean (exc. Elect)	154	114	135	167	121	134	124	106	132	112

(a)Excludes electricity.

to skewness. But, for all of these reasons the relationships which emerge from this study should be regarded as tentative and suggestive of broad trends rather than precise formulations of stable and exact relationships. Finally, some relations between the variables were obscured when all industries were used as observations. Consequently, a separate analysis was conducted for (*a*) transportable goods industries including building and construction and electricity (*b*) food industries (including drink) and (*c*) industries other than food. Thus there are three parts to Table 5·2 which sets out the correlation coefficients

TABLE 5·2

Correlation coefficients for movements of selected variables

Product moment correlations between movements of:	for all industries r=	for food industries r=	for industries other than food r=
Earnings per operative & output per operative	−0·05	−0·13	−0·12
Unit wage cost & output per operative	−0·88	−0·95	−0·84
Unit labour cost & output per head	−0·86	−0·85	−0·83
Unit labour cost & unit gross margin cost	+0·16	−0·39	+0·44
Output per head & unit gross margin cost	−0·15	+0·18	−0·36
Output per head & unit material cost	−0·11	−0·27	−0·22
Unit labour cost & unit material cost	+0·08	+0·14	+0·27
Gross prices & output per head	−0·38	−0·32	−0·50
Gross prices & unit labour cost	+0·43	+0·19	+0·61
Gross prices & unit gross margin cost	+0·46	+0·01	+0·54
Gross prices & unit material cost	+0·86	+0·82	+0·86
Gross prices & gross output	−0·11	−0·29	−0·12
Unit material cost & gross output	+0·11	−0·11	+0·11
Output per head & gross output	+0·56	+0·18	+0·48
Employment & gross output	+0·77	+0·78	+0·87
Employment & output per head	−0·09	−0·44	−0·03
Gross output & unit gross margin cost	−0·31	−0·34	−0·43
Gross output & unit labour cost	−0·46	·00	−0·40

For all industries [50 observations] r=0·28 is significant at the 5% confidence level.

For industries other than food [36 observations] r=0·32 is significant at the 5% confidence level.

For food industries [14 observations] r=0·53 is significant at the 5% confidence level.

obtained by correlating the movements of the variables with each other, each industry being treated as an observation.

Looking first at the overall pattern of output, cost and productivity movements it is apparent from Table 5·1 that output has shown the greatest diversity of movement followed by unit gross margin cost, employment, unit wage and labour costs and output per head. Two industries—fertilisers and electrical machinery—have more than doubled output while seven—cocoa and sugar confectionery, bread and flour confectionery, grain milling, distilling, men's and boys' clothing, and railroad equipment—have recorded absolute decline. And, although three industries have managed to more than double their labour force, perhaps most striking of all is the fact that 13 industries—or more than one quarter of the total—have experienced an absolute fall in employment. Among the variables with a relatively low degree of dispersion earnings per operative, unit material cost, and price are the most prominent.

5.4 Earnings per operative and output per operative

From the more detailed breakdown in Table 5·3 of changes in each of these variables, it is obvious that variations in earnings per operative have been considerably less than variations

TABLE 5·3

Frequency distributions of percentage changes (1953–63) in earnings per operative and operative productivity[a]

	200– over	199– 180	179– 160	159– 140	139– 120	119– 100	99– 80	79– under	total
Earnings per operative	2	6	33	7	1				49
Output per operative	2		8	14	11	5	6	3	49

	lower quartile	median	upper quartile	
Earnings per operative	174·5	167	160·5	} Index to base
Output per operative	110·1	136	155·0	} 1953＝100

(a) Electricity is excluded due to lack of data.

in output per operative. It is also quite clear that earnings have been increasing at a more rapid rate than operative productivity which would imply that increases in earnings have been independent of the level of productivity and indeed the near zero correlations in Table 5·2 confirm the lack of any relationship between movements of the two variables. In other words, there is no tendency for greater than average increases in productivity to be accompanied by greater than average increases in earnings. A similar conclusion was reached by Salter in his study of U.K. industries. It means, in effect, that industry wages are determined by factors other than the level of productivity, and that such factors are common to all industries. Salter argues that the movement of wages in each industry is primarily determined by the movement of wages in the economy as a whole since the labour market is common to all industries. In Ireland, there is at least one additional factor. Such evidence as is available suggests that there is a long run tendency for wages in Ireland and the U.K. to change at more or less similar rates, a tendency which is ascribed to the essential unity of the British and Irish labour markets. (35) To the extent that this is true, it means that wage rates in Ireland are more closely tied to changes in British rates than to changes in Irish labour productivity.

5.5 Labour productivity and unit labour costs

Since earnings increases are unrelated to productivity performance, variations in unit labour costs may rise because of the unequal distribution of productivity increases among industries. Indeed, six industries have nearly doubled their unit labour costs showing that increases in wages and salaries were not absorbed by higher levels of productivity, while a further six have achieved absolute reductions indicating a net saving of labour per unit of output. Turning to Table 5·2, the correlation coefficients for movements of labour productivity and unit labour costs range from −0·83 to −0·95. These strong negative relationships indicate that industries with the largest increases in labour productivity have had the smallest unit labour cost increases. And conversely, industries with below average increases in productivity have had above average increases in labour costs. Thus, inter-industry variations in productivity result in similar but inverse variations in unit labour costs.

5.6 Labour productivity and gross margin costs

As may be seen from Table 5·2 a number of distinct patterns emerge when different groupings of the variables are considered. First, among all industries there is no relation between the movements of either unit labour costs and unit gross margin costs $(r = +0·16)$ or between labour productivity and unit gross margin cost $(r = -0·15)$.[4] Nor is there any significant relation when the food industries alone are analysed. This means that there is no global tendency for industries with below average increases in unit labour costs or above average increases in productivity to have below average increases in unit gross margin costs. On the other hand, for industries other than food, there is evidence of a positive and significant association between movements of labour costs and gross margin costs, and a negative and significant association between the latter and labour productivity. These relations indicate that among these industries those with the smallest increases in unit labour costs and the largest increases in productivity tend to register the smallest increases in unit gross margin costs, while in contrast, industries with the lowest productivity increases tend to the greatest increases in unit margin costs.

5.7 Labour productivity and unit material costs

There is no relationship between unit material cost and labour productivity or between unit material cost and unit labour cost. Indeed, the correlation coefficients are too small even to suggest an association. As a result, there is no tendency for industries with greater than average increases in productivity and savings in labour cost to achieve greater than average savings in unit material costs, nor do industries with below average increases in productivity incur greater than average

[4]Among U.K. industries, Salter found a positive and significant correlation for movements of unit labour cost and unit gross margin cost, and a negative and significant correlation for movements of unit gross margin cost and labour productivity.

increases in material costs. Again, this result is in striking contrast to the findings of Salter whose study of U.K. and U.S. industries reveals a strong negative association between labour productivity and unit material cost. Indeed, at industry level in the two countries differential movements of labour productivity are associated with differential movements in all elements of cost so that industries with above average increases in productivity tend to have below average increases in unit labour, unit gross margin and unit material costs. The reasons why similar relationships do not exist among Irish industries will be discussed later.

A quick review of the relationships arising out of the variations of labour productivity and the components of cost shows that the only significant relation holding for all industry groupings is that between labour productivity and unit labour costs. The relation between unit gross margin cost and productivity is more complex. While no relation exists among all industries or among the food industries a significant association does exist among industries other than food. And finally, no relation of any description can be detected for movements of labour productivity and unit material cost.

It seems, therefore, that the impact of changes in productivity on the structure of industry costs is fairly limited among the food industries, affecting labour costs alone. Among all other industries the impact is more widespread since here above average savings in labour costs as a result of above average increases in productivity are augmented by concomitant above average savings in unit margin costs.

5.8 Gross prices and labour productivity

Gross price has three constituent elements—unit gross margin cost, unit labour cost and unit material cost. Consequently, variations of gross price must be reflected in compensating variations of at least one of these three variables. It comes as no surprise, then, that movements of gross price are significantly related to movements of each of its components (Table 5·2).[5]

[5]With the exception of movements of unit labour cost and gross prices and unit margin cost and gross prices among the food industries.

The question posed, therefore, is whether movements of labour productivity are related to movements of gross prices, and, if so, to what extent.

The first part of the question is easily answered. From Table 5·2 it is clear that a significant and negative relation exists between movements of both variables among all industries and industries other than food but not among the food industries. Thus, while there is a general tendency for above average increases in productivity to be associated with below average increases in relative prices it appears that movements of labour productivity do not have much impact on the price levels of the food industries.

One reason for the associations is not too difficult to find. Further reference to Table 5·2 shows that even stronger relationships exist between movements of unit labour costs and gross prices among industries in all groups except food. Recalling, then, that differential movements of labour productivity are associated with differential movements of unit labour cost, it appears that the relation between these two variables and the relation between unit labour cost and gross prices explain at least partially the observed relationship between labour productivity and gross prices.

Some estimate of the strength of this relationship may be gauged from the magnitude of the correlation coefficients. For example, the coefficient of −0·38 for movements of prices and labour productivity among all industries suggests that here 14 per cent of the variation in relative prices can be explained by variations in labour productivity alone. And, similarly movements of labour productivity can account for 25 per cent of the relative price variation among industries other than food. It is also instructive to examine the equation for the regression of movements of gross prices on movements of labour productivity for industries other than food. This is given by:

$$Y = 199·5 - 0·54X \quad (S.E. = 0·17)$$

where Y and X are the movements of gross prices and labour productivity respectively and S.E. is the standard error of the regression coefficient. It suggests that, on average, a 10 per cent increase in labour productivity leads to a 5·4 per cent decrease in gross prices. Although the regression coefficient is not overly large by any absolute criterion it is in fact well beyond the range which would be expected considering that unit labour costs comprise on the average no more than 20 per cent of total costs. It appears implausible, therefore, to explain it in terms of savings in labour usage alone. Rather, it reflects the interaction of differential movements of labour productivity with differential movements of both unit labour and gross margin costs. Thus the proportion of the variation in relative price which can be explained by movements of labour productivity is more or less commensurate with labour's share only among all industries for here productivity is associated with unit labour costs alone. Among industries other than food, movements of labour productivity are associated with two constituents of cost which are in turn associated with gross prices so that the increase in relative prices as a result of an increase in productivity is less than would be the case were movements of productivity related solely to movements of unit labour costs.

5.9 Gross prices and unit material costs

Even though the preceding analysis indicates that changes in unit labour and unit gross margin costs are significantly correlated with changes in gross prices among all industries and industries other than food, the overall influence of these two variables is not very strong. At best, among industries other than food, variations of unit labour cost can account for 36 per cent, and variations of unit gross margin costs for 28 per cent of relative price changes. It is not surprising, therefore, that movements of the final component of cost-unit material cost—are highly correlated with movements of gross price, the correlation coefficients ranging from +0·86 among all industries, and industries other than food, to +0·82 among the food industries. Indeed, this latter figure underestimates the degree of the relation among the food industries proper. For, when all the drink industries (which have a lower material content per unit of output than the food industries proper) are excluded, the rank correlation coefficient for movements of the two variables becomes unity. But even so, the overwhelming influence of material costs on prices may be readily ascertained. First, changes in unit material cost can explain 74 per cent of the changes in gross prices among all industries and industries other than food, and 67 per cent of changes in gross prices among the food industries. Second, the regression of movements of gross prices on movements of unit material cost produces the equation;

$$Y = 67 \cdot 5 + 0 \cdot 67X \quad (S.E. = 0 \cdot 07)$$

for industries other than food where Y and X are the movements of gross prices and unit material cost respectively. The equation suggests that a 10 per cent increase in unit material costs will lead to a 6·7 per cent increase in gross prices.

The very high interrelation between movements of prices and unit material costs, and the sizes of the correlation coefficients reflect primarily the structure of industrial output, a structure typified by the low degree of fabrication to which materials are subjected in industrial processes. This is more apparent from Table 5·4. There are only 14 industries in which the net output content of gross output exceeds 50 per cent. Over all industries material costs come to 68 per cent of selling price, labour costs to 17 per cent and gross margin costs to 15 per cent. This domination of the cost structure by the material content is even more pronounced among the food industries. Here material inputs account for 75 per cent of total costs in five industries and between 60 per cent and 70 per cent in another five. Thus, the absence of any significant relation between labour productivity and prices, between unit labour cost and prices, and between unit gross margin cost and prices may simply reflect the fact that gross margins and labour each constitute a small proportion of total costs. Accordingly, even if considerable savings in these costs were realised, they would account for either a minute proportion of selling price or could be offset by slight changes in material costs. And although the material component of cost is not so large as to prevent movements in labour productivity, unit labour and unit gross margin costs from having an impact on price levels among industries other than food, it is still large enough to curtail severely the strength of such relations.

TABLE 5·4

Frequency distribution of percentage cost components of gross output, 1963

Percentage distribution	distribution of industries according to cost structure		
	material costs	labour costs	gross margin costs
0–9	—	6	7
10–19	—	14	23
20–29	4	17	11
30–39	6	6	4
40–49	4	2	1
50–59	8	—	2
60–69	16	3	—
70–79	5	—	—
80–89	4	—	—
90 & over	1	—	—

	percentage average		
Manufacturing industry	69	16	15
Transportable goods	68	17	15

5.10 Gross prices and gross output

Normally it would be expected that industries with above average rates of growth would tend to have below average price increases due to economies of scale and the introduction of cost saving capital techniques etc. It would also seem that the converse should hold, namely, that industries with below average price increases should expand rapidly due to the stimulation of demand. Indeed, a significant association between differential movements of prices and output has been found in a number of studies (36, 33) an association which is regarded as one of the factors promoting economic growth.

In view of this the correlation coefficients for movements of the two variables are somewhat disconcerting since they are not significant no matter what industry grouping is employed. It appears therefore that there is no tendency for industries with the largest increases in output to record the smallest increases in relative prices nor for industries which are relatively stagnant to record above average price increases.

There are, however, a number of reasons for the observed discrepancy between the behaviour of the variables among Irish industries, and their more usual behaviour as exhibited, say, among U.K. and U.S. industries.

First, there is the question of what determines changes in material costs. It may be recalled from the discussion in 1.10 that industries in developed economies are linked together as output-users and input-producers. Now, in this context the major material cost savings which accrue to an industry as a result of rapid expansion tend to come not from the economies of bulk handling or purchasing but rather from the economies achieved in the input producing industries as a result of their induced expansion. Thus, allowing only, for example, that above average increases in labour productivity are associated with below average price increases, then any increase in productivity in the input producing industry as a result of the rapid expansion of demand in the industry using its output as input will result in below average price increases in the former and hence in a relatively cheaper input for the latter.

With the exception of the food industries most Irish industries import their raw materials. Hence, the relevant material price levels are not those of domestic supply industries but rather those of foreign industries, and relative price variations are associated with productivity and output movements of industries in the exporting countries concerned. In addition, because of their small absolute sizes Irish industries are in the position of marginal purchasers so that even large increases in their demands would have no more than a negligible impact on the output and price performance of the foreign-based supply industries. To a large extent, therefore, material prices are exogenous to the Irish economic system, being almost totally beyond the control of domestic industries and their rates of expansion. Accordingly, the absence of any relationship between differential movements of output and unit material cost (Table 5·2) should come as no surprise. Nor for that matter should the lack of an association between differential movements of labour productivity and unit material cost. For again it reiterates the point that the price components of unit material cost are determined by forces extraneous to the Irish economic system, and completely unrelated to its performance.

A second explanation is particularly relevant to the food industries but is also generally applicable. Many Irish industries export a considerable portion of their output and for these industries the relevant price criterion is not the relative movements of gross prices in domestic industries but rather the variation of prices in those industries which compete in their export markets. It is quite conceivable, for example, that an export-oriented industry may record a below average increase in prices *vis-à-vis* other domestic industries which is at the same time an above average increase *vis-à-vis* the industries with which it is competing in export markets. In such a situation there would certainly be little stimulus for expansion.

What general conclusions may be drawn? It seems that increases in labour productivity and associated saving in non-material costs do not have a very strong effect on the price level. Nor is it safe to assume that they will have an effect until the structure of output becomes more interdependent. This of course will depend on the achievement of higher levels of processing and fabrication so that labour and capital costs account for higher proportions of gross output than at present. In addition, the price component of the principal cost variable associated with gross prices—unit material cost—is by and large an exogenous variable. As a result, variations of industry prices are, to a considerable extent, beyond the control of the Irish manufacturers. It would, perhaps, be possible to alleviate some of the impact of these factors were manufacturers to become more aware of alternative sources of materials, more willing to seek substitutes, and most important of all, more diligent in their efforts to promote higher levels of productivity and efficiency in the purchase, handling and processing of material inputs.

5.11 Gross output and labour productivity

The correlation coefficients indicate two distinct trends. First, among all industries, and industries other than food, there is a significant tendency for higher than average increases in output to accompany higher than average increases in productivity. A similar relation has been found in numerous other studies (50, 36, 33, 34, 51) and of the explanatory hypotheses put forward two will be briefly mentioned here. On the one hand, large advances in labour productivity may be brought about by economies of scale etc. which result from a rapid expansion of demand and output. On the other hand, increases in productivity which lead to a fall in relative prices may stimulate demand, and consequently induce higher levels of output. However, since it has been seen that the price levels react weakly to changes in labour productivity, and that output is unresponsive to relative price variations, it is more likely that some aspect of output growth induces increases in productivity.

The behaviour of the variables among the food industries is once again contrary to the overall experience. Differential movements of gross output are not associated with differential movements of labour productivity so that here above average rates of output growth do not induce above average increases in productivity.

5.12 Gross output, productivity and employment

Reference to Table 5.2 shows that in all industry groupings there is a significant correlation between movements of gross output and employment. This indicates that industries with the most rapid growth account for the largest increases in employment while below average growers experience below average employment increases. On the other hand, among all industries, and industries other than food, there is no direct association between increases in labour productivity and employment. Thus, although rising labour productivity implies an economy in labour input per unit of output it seems that that does not adversely affect the demand for labour in industries with large productivity gains, mainly because these industries are also the most rapid growers. However, among the food industries this is not so. Here the negative correlation coefficient is almost significant, and would suggest that there is in fact a tendency for industries with the largest increases in labour productivity to record the smallest increases in employment.

5.13 Productivity and economic growth

Before attempting to explain why the relationships noted in the preceding sections have arisen it is worth while examining the manner in which the global interaction of the variables can affect economic growth.

There are, of course, many growth models differing in structure and underlying assumptions. Two of the more well known types are those which are supply determined, and those demand determined. The former, as their designation would suggest, postulate that growth is primarily determined by factors operating on the supply side. That is to say, by the rates of growth of the labour force, of the capital stock, and of technical progress which is often treated as an exogenously given rate of growth of productivity. It is assumed, therefore, that all that can be produced will be consumed i.e. that supply creates its own demand. Indeed, most models incorporate specific mechanisms, such as flexible price levels etc., to ensure that markets are in fact always cleared.

A demand model on the other hand specifies that the rate of growth of potential output is a function of the rate of growth of demand. Here it is assumed that there are no constraints on the supply side, supply automatically adjusts to demand i.e. supply is elastic. This assumption is retained in the schematic description of the growth process which follows: it is by no means an unreasonable premise as long as the growth rate lies within prudent limits. At very high rates of growth supply constraints would, of course, put a ceiling on further expansion.

Every economy is characterised by a structure of products and industries which are at different stages of their life cycles. Typically, a new product comes on the market as a luxury item, the income elasticity of demand is greater than unity so that a 1 per cent increase in income results in a more than 1 per cent increase in demand. In other words, luxury items have a rapid growth potential given a rapid growth of income. However, with the passage of time, and the continued growth of income, income elasticities of demand begin to fall, products move out of the luxury classes, demand responds more sluggishly to changes in income until finally the products become necessities. At this point demand tends to be unreceptive to further increases in income and eventually the manufacturing industries concerned become stagnant, or even decline. Thus, crude though the analogy may sound, products are in a sense similar to people. In the early stages of their life cycle growth is rapid, a period of maturity follows, then a slow succumbing to senility, and finally death.

Economic growth may be viewed, therefore, as a sequence of movements through a hierarchy of goods.[6] At any point in time some products are stagnant or declining, some are necessities and others still are luxuries. As income continues to increase the stagnant and declining products may cease to be produced, some necessities enter the stagnant and declining phase, luxuries become necessities and new products take the place of the former luxuries. In other words, growth is an unbalanced process. Given, then, a rapid rate of growth of aggregate demand it follows that the composition of demand will also change rapidly, and hence the composition of output.

The industries which are expanding rapidly will enjoy above average increases in productivity and reductions in cost. One way in which cost reductions may be realised is through the impact of a rapid rate of growth of demand on the kind of technology employed in an industry. For, contrary to the traditional assumption of economic theory which envisions smooth isoquants and the continuous substitutability of labour and capital, there is usually only a limited number of ways in which a firm may combine labour and capital. The choice very often is between techniques which are inherently labour intensive and those which are highly capital intensive. Accordingly, whether or not a firm will move from the former to the latter depends not on the actual level of demand but on its rate of growth. Very rapid growth may erase the cost prohibiting barriers associated with capital indivisibilities etc. and

[6]Cf. Cornwall 'The role of investment demand in long run growth' (57).

thus lead to the introduction of capital intensive techniques.

The important point, however, is this: the more rapid the movement through a hierarchy of goods, the more rapid the changes in the composition of output, and consequently the more rapid the achievement of above average increases in productivity in individual industries. And the more rapid this latter process the higher the average level of productivity and income. But just how rapidly the actual movement through a hierarchy of goods occurs depends on factors besides the rate of growth of aggregate demand.

First, there are the relations between movements of productivity and costs, and output and prices. If above average increases in productivity are associated with below average increases in all elements of cost so that rapid growth industries incur below average price increases then the process of movement is speeded up. For growth of demand is a function of price and income elasticities. Accordingly, when differential increases in output and productivity are associated with differential movements of prices, demand tends to shift from industries experiencing above average price increases to those experiencing below average price increases or, in the present context, from the slow growers to the rapid growers. Thus, unbalanced growth may create the very conditions which lead to even greater imbalance in the growth process.

A second contributory factor is the relationship between the rate of growth of demand, and the rate of transfer of resources. It has already been established that rapid growth industries tend to sustain the largest increases in employment. In other studies an even more important relationship has been found, namely, that industries with above average increases in productivity have above average increases in employment. And since industries with rapid rates of growth either are, or become, industries with above average levels of productivity, the movement of labour or resources in general from slow growth industries to rapid growth ones leads inevitably to a higher overall average level of productivity. Indeed, the growth of productivity, whether it be that of labour or of all factors, can be disaggregated into two components: the growth which is due to the reallocation of resources between industries (the inter-industry element), and the growth which occurs within industries (the intra-industry element). Even if there were no increase in productivity within individual industries there would nevertheless be an increase in the overall average level of productivity provided that the average levels of productivity were higher in those industries to which resources moved than the average levels of productivity in the industries from whence they came. The importance of resource reallocation as an instrument of productivity growth cannot be overstressed. Salter estimates that it accounted for almost one-half of labour productivity advances in U.K. industries between 1924 and 1950, while a disaggregation of total factor productivity growth between 1947 and 1957 in the U.S. suggests that one-third of the growth may be attributed to inter-industry resource movements. (52) But the willingness of labour to move, and of entrepreneurs to invest, depends to a large extent on the economic environment. The unemployment rate, for instance, should be either stabilised or declining, or otherwise trade unions are likely to be unreceptive to innovations, and entrepreneurs wary of investments. Furthermore, declining industries should not be subsidised, economic and social institutions should be adaptable to change, and placement bureaus and job re-training programmes should be organised efficiently, etc.

Finally, product life cycles are affected by the level of inter-industry relations. The role of this factor in the growth process has been described in 1·10, the economic consequences of specialisation in 3·3, and the association between industry linkages and movements of prices and gross output in 5·10. The kernel of the argument may be stated simply. A high level of inter-industry relations strengthens the associations between movements of productivity, output, costs, prices and employment. Thus, other things being equal, a given rate of growth of demand will give rise to a larger increase in the overall average level of productivity and income the more sophisticated the level of inter-industry relations.

It only remains to be said that since Ireland is an open economy heavily reliant on imports and exports, and is also in the middle stages of development, the impact of the growth process just described is dampened because the first and third factors operate only to a limited extent, if at all.

5.14 Conclusion

Increasing productivity, as noted in the introduction, is an essential of economic growth. This chapter set out, therefore, to provide, first, an understanding of what productivity measurement is all about. This proved to be a fairly complicated task since it was found that many of the problems encountered are highly intricate, and present formidable methodological and operational difficulties. Indeed, the usual measure of productivity—an index of volume gross output per man hour or man year—has few of the qualities considered desirable in an index. Besides, it is misleading to speak of the productivity of a single factor since it is quite possible for an increase in the productivity of labour, for example, to be offset by a fall in the productivity of other factors. Adding to the confusion is the tendency to regard increasing productivity as being synonymous with increasing efficiency in resource use. There is, of course, no relation between the two variables, and productivity has no connection at all with efficiency.

Following the discussion of input, output and productivity, an inter-industry analysis of productivity, output, cost, price and employment movements between 1953 and 1963 was carried out. Here the purpose was to ascertain what relations, if any, existed between the relative movements of the variables. The conclusions which emerged from the study were as follows: first, among industries other than food there are significant relations between movements of labour productivity and unit gross margin costs, labour productivity and gross output, gross prices and unit material costs, and gross output and employment; second among the food industries the number of significant relations is far more limited, associations existing only for movements of labour productivity and unit labour costs, gross prices and unit material costs, and gross output and employment.

The overall findings are similar to the results of other studies except in two important respects—there are no significant relations between either the movements of labour productivity and unit material cost, or between movement of gross output and prices. The aberrant behaviour of the variables in these instances is primarily due to the interaction of two factors. First, prices are dominated by their unit material cost content, and second, imports account for the bulk of materials used in Irish manufacturing industries. Accordingly, material costs are to a large degree an exogenous variable over which domestic manufacturers can exercise little or no control.

In the final section the role of productivity, output, cost, price and employment interrelationships as agents of economic growth was discussed. And, it appears that the stronger these relationships the greater the growth potential.

6 INTER-INDUSTRY RELATIONS: AN EXPLANATION

6.1 Introduction

In this chapter the reasons for the inter-industry relations observed in Chapter 5 will be discussed.

As a first step, consider what may cause an increase in the productivity of labour. First, there is the increased personal efficiency of labour. However, for a variety of reasons this factor is regarded by economists as being of little significance, and it certainly would be implausible to ascribe differential changes in labour productivity among industries primarily to variations in either the quality or the intensity of the work effort of their labour forces. This leaves factor substitution and technological progress. The former speaks for itself—the substitution of capital for labour increases the marginal productivity of labour and diminishes the marginal productivity of capital. Turning then, to technological progress, the first thing to recognise is its identity with total factor productivity measures. It will be recalled that in this sense, productivity refers to output per unit composite input, and that the rate of growth of productivity is the rate of growth of output per unit input. Now, since an increase in production can occur only in the event of either an increase in the supply of factors or an increase in their productive capacity, the latter being attributed to technological progress, it follows that the first type is explicitly taken care of in a total factor productivity measure since its components are enumerated in the production index and the input index. What a total factor index measures, therefore, is the change in output (per unit input) which cannot be explained by increased availability of factors, or, in other words, the change due to technological progress. [1]

[1]Technological progress has also been referred to at one time or another as the 'residual' or, most appropriately perhaps, as 'a measure of our ignorance'.

Two definitions will illustrate just how imprecise this term is. E. E. Hagen, judges it to embrace 'the discovery of new knowledge which makes possible an increase in the output of goods and services per unit of labour, capital and materials used in production, and the incorporation of that knowledge in productive processes. It includes the provision of more satisfying products as well as more efficient methods of production. It includes the entire process of innovation from an advance in pure science to its adoption in engineering and its application in production. Within the realms of methods it represents not only scientific and technical advance but also the devising of new forms of organisation or methods of procedure which make society more efficient in production'; (38) for another writer it covers 'not just technological progress alone but also a whole group of actions consisting of technological progress in the narrow sense; economies of scale; external economies; improved health; education and skill of the labour force, better management and changes in product mix'. (39) One can distinguish, therefore, between pure technical progress, which consists of the application of science to industry, extending the range of production possibilities, and the introduction of new products and processes, and the broader, more sweeping type already described.

But whatever ambiguity there may be regarding the scope and character of technological progress, there is considerable evidence to show that it, rather than capital formation, is the main determinant of increasing labour productivity. Indeed, one study estimated that it accounted for at least 86 per cent of the per capita increase in the G.N.P. of the U.S. between 1879 and 1950. (40) However, it must also be recognised that studies of this nature understate the importance of capital since measures of capital have a downward bias because they fail to take account of quality improvements; and technological progress is functionally related in some way to the rate of capital formation. The question therefore, which will be examined in this chapter is whether the inter-industry relations observed can be explained in terms of factor substitution and some or all of the various elements of technological progress. And it should be borne in mind that for the explanation to be satisfactory, it must reconcile the differences between the behaviour of the food industries and industries other than food.

6.2 Factor substitution

The substitution of capital for labour may occur in the wake of a rise in the price of labour relative to that of capital. However, since such movements in factor prices are general for all industries, the mere act of substitution cannot, as Salter pointed out, account for inter-industry variations in productivity growth. Accordingly, if factor substitution is to remain useful as an explanatory variable the argument for it must be reframed in terms which are compatible with differential productivity gains. Consequently, there must be inter-industry variations in the ease with which capital can be substituted for labour, i.e. there must be variations among industries in the elasticity of substitution. On this basis, the less difficulty there is in substituting capital for labour, the higher the elasticity of substitution and the greater the increase in labour productivity.

This hypothesis however, has an important corollary. It implies that the industries with the largest savings in labour costs will record the largest increases in capital costs. Unfortunately, the only indicator of capital costs is unit gross margin cost. However, despite its crudity and imperfection there should, if the hypothesis is correct, be at least some slight associations between movements of labour productivity and unit gross margin cost and between unit labour cost and unit gross margin cost.

Referring back to Table 5·2, it appears that in both respects the behaviour of the food and all other industries is divergent. First, among the food group there is a correlation of −0·39 for movements of unit labour costs and unit gross margin costs, and of +0·18 for movements of labour productivity and unit margins. While neither of these coefficients is significant, the first is not too far off and suggests that there is a slight tendency for above average savings in labour costs to be associated with above average increases in unit gross margin costs. While the second correlation provides no useful information, the association between labour productivity and gross margin cost can be approached from another angle. In Table 6·1, the food industries are ranked on the basis of relative changes in productivity and percentage changes in the share of gross margin

TABLE 6·1

Percentage changes in relative cost shares between 1953 and 1963

Industry	productivity	per cent changes in relative shares		
		% materials	% labour costs	% gross margin costs
Soft drinks	145	−10	+10	+21
Butter-blending & margarine	140	−15	+33	+77
Malting	134	−15	+36	+46
Dairy products	125		+25	−14
Distilling	116	−30	+13	+133
Slaughtering etc.	115	−2	+25	+12
Brewing	109	−39	+31	+34
Grain-milling & AFS	108	−5	+33	+33
Bread & biscuits	103	−3	+5	+6
Bacon factories	97	−3	+40	+17
Sugar, cocoa, chocolate & sugar confectionery	89	−9	+70	—
Canning of fruit & vegetables	74	−6	+39	−6
Miscellaneous food preparations	73	−17	+100	+33

For movements of productivity & percentage change in the relative share of gross margin costs r=0·55 is significant at the 5% confidence level.

in net output. The rank correlation for movements of both variables is +0·37, and although not significant for 13 observations, it does become so when one extreme observation—miscellaneous food preparations—is excluded and the correlation rises to +0·57. This would suggest that the food industries recording the largest increases in productivity were those in which the share of gross margin in net output was increasing most rapidly. It appears then, on the basis of this preliminary investigation, that, insofar as unit gross margin cost and the share of gross margin in net output can be taken as approximations of capital costs, the behaviour of the food industries conforms to the hypothesis that differential increases in productivity may be explained by differences between industries in the elasticity of substitution.

But this is by no means the case among industries other than food. Here the correlations of $+0.44$ for movements of unit labour costs and gross margins, and of -0.36 for labour productivity and gross margins are both significant and suggest, first, that above average savings in labour costs are associated with above average savings in gross margin costs, and second, that above average increases in productivity are associated with below average increases in gross margin costs. Thus, if factor substitution occurred along the lines suggested in these industries, it is apparent that its effects on the structure of labour and capital costs have been eroded by the impact of other factors. Salter identifies two—economies of scale (both internal and external) and technical change (defined in the more limited way as a shift in the production function as a result of new knowledge easing technical constraints and opening up a superior range of production possibilities).(33) Indeed, the inter-industry relations among U.K. and U.S. industries are due, he argues, to the uneven impact of these factors superimposed on factor substitution. If a somewhat similar argument is made for inter-industry relations in Ireland it must be shown, first, that the food industries were not characterised by tendencies to exploit economies of scale, second, that they did not enjoy the benefits of a high rate of technical advance; and finally, that the relatively strong impact of both factors on industries other than food led to the associations already noted.

6.3 Economies of scale

By now it should be clear that the opportunities for realising economies of scale are closely related to the rate of market expansion. One yard-stick of the latter is the rate of output growth and it may reasonably be expected that the higher the rate of growth of output the greater the opportunities for realising economies of scale. Using this criterion, it is interesting to contrast the overall experiences which the food and all other industries have had during the decade under review. (Table 6·2). First, the food industries recorded below average increases

TABLE 6·2

Movements in output & cost for all industries, food industries and industries other than food (index to base 1953 = 100).

		industries	
	all industries	food industries	other than food
Volume output	157	114	175
Employment	113	108	121
Output per head	139	106	145
Operatives	112	107	118
Output per operative	138	107	148
Earnings per operative	167	164	170
Unit wage cost	121	153	115
Unit labour cost	121	155	117
Unit gross margin cost	134	137	132
Unit material cost	106	114	105
Gross prices	112	120	111

NOTE: Electricity is not included in indexes for operatives, output per operative, earnings per operative & unit wage cost.

in output growth, employment, productivity and above average increases in all elements of cost and gross prices. Second, in industries other than food, the increase in output was 53 per cent greater than the increase in the food industries, the employment increase 26 per cent greater, the productivity gain 75 per cent greater while the increase in unit labour costs came to less than 30 per cent of the increase in the food industries. Third, reviewing the relative performance of the nine major industry groupings (Table 6·3) the food group ranked lowest on output increase, second lowest on employment gains, while also recording the largest unit labour cost increase, the fourth largest unit margin cost increase, the third largest unit material cost increase and the fourth largest price increase. And finally, whereas the food group had a simple average rate of growth of

TABLE 6·3

Movements in cost & output in other industry groupings (index to base 1953=100).

	textiles	clothing & footwear	wood & furniture	paper & printing	chemi-cals	clay & glass	metal & engine-ering	mining & turf
Volume output	189	141	133	169	212	182	257	207
Employment	124	104	88	118	141	129	151	124
Output per head	152	136	151	143	150	141	170	167
Operatives	120	103	88	114	134	126	149	125
Output per operative	158	137	151	148	158	144	172	166
Earnings per operative	176	159	153	182	160	175	162	182
Unit wage cost	111	116	101	123	101	122	94	110
Unit labour cost	115	119	103	125	108	124	95	111
Unit gross margin cost	100	150	138	123	158	180	126	116
Unit material cost	97	103	91	123	98	100	113	123
Gross price	101	113	100	124	109	124	126	115

1·4 per cent per annum, all other industries had a rate of 7·5 per cent per annum, which means that their markets were expanding more than five times as rapidly. On almost every count, therefore, the food industries were either stagnating or lagging well behind the performances of other industries.

A further argument for the 'factor-substitution-only' thesis in the food industries is provided by the behaviour of relative movements of productivity and employment. The correlation is −0·44 which is almost significant, and at least suggestive of a tendency for industries with the largest increases in labour productivity to have above average reductions or below average increases in employment. On the other hand, the expansion of output has had singularly little impact on the structure of costs. Above average expansion did not lead to above average increases in productivity or to below average increases in unit gross margin and unit labour costs. (Table 5·2)

However, the empirical findings are perfectly consistent with the hypothesis that among industries other than food rapid growers enjoyed economies of scale, and hence the positive and significant association between movements of gross output and labour productivity ($r = +0\cdot48$), and the negative and significant associations for gross output and unit margin cost ($r = -0\cdot43$), and gross output and unit labour costs ($r = -0\cdot40$).

There is one final point which should be made. It was seen earlier that no relation exists between relative movements of labour productivity and earnings per head, and that consequently wage increases were attributed to factors common to all industries. It is little wonder then, that factor substitution emerges as the principle determinant of increasing labour productivity in the food industries. For these industries incurred the largest increases in unit labour costs because, both as a group and individually, they recorded below average increases in productivity compared with all other industries. Moreover, among the food industries those registering the highest productivity gains and savings in labour costs were not usually the most rapidly expanding. This means that factor substitution took place in the face of slowly rising, static or even declining output. It seems, therefore, that the upward pressure of wages, largely exogenous and resulting in, or implying, exorbitant increases in the unit labour costs of the food industries induced factor substitution.

6.4 Technical change

Although an explanation in terms of factor substitution and economies of scale by itself provides a rational interpretation of the inter-industry relations this explanation can be made much clearer by examining the role of technical change in the process. The thesis offered is that the uneven impact of technical change on industries has stimulated uneven movements in labour productivity, output, and the structure of labour and capital costs. If this thesis is correct, then it must be shown, first, that the food industries experienced a relatively low level of technical change; and, second, that industries with the largest increases in output and productivity and the smallest increases in costs were technologically the most progressive.

Since technical change is a component of innovating activity a close connection between technical change and the

8

research and development (R & D) outlays of industries comes as no surprise. Estimates of R & D for eleven Irish industry groups were compiled for the Report on Science and Irish Economic Development, and are presented in Table 6·4. Most

TABLE 6·4

Research and development expenditure and output and productivity performance in industry groupings

Industry	R+D expenditure 1963 (£000)	volume output 1963	productivity 1963
Food (food & drink)	401·7	114	106
Metal & engineering	202·8	257	170
Mining & turf	81·8	207	167
Other manufactures (a)	51·6	252	181
Chemicals	44·0	212	150
Glass, clay & cement	27·6	182	141
Clothing & footwear	26·4	141	136
Building & construction	26·2	136	153
Textiles	23·8	189	152
Printing & publishing	20·1	169	143
Wood & cork	0·8	133	151

(a) Includes miscellaneous manufacture, fellmongery & leather goods.

striking is the overwhelming preponderance of R&D in the food industries, which would suggest at least superficially that they were indeed the most technically progressive. But as regards significant associations between levels of R&D expenditure and the growth of output and productivity two distinct patterns emerge. First, there are no associations of any magnitude over all industries. But when the food group is excluded a significant relation does emerge between R&D expenditure and the growth of output— $r = +0·82$ —and an almost significant relation between R&D expenditure and productivity— $r = +0·50$ —(for significance $r = +·63$). Thus, to the extent that R&D expenditure is an indicator of technical progress there are some grounds for arguing that in industries other than food higher levels of technical progress were accompanied by larger increases in output and productivity.

However, it is doubtful whether R&D expenditure contributed much to the level of technical change during the decade. To understand why, it is necessary to examine the nature of technological progress and the structural prerequisites of an economic system which foster the growth of technology. Once again, inter-industry linkages and the level of specialisation, especially in the capital goods sector, assume basic roles. In order to simplify what is in fact an extraordinarily complex subject, the present analysis will be confined to a brief discussion of some of the more important determinants of technological advances.

A useful starting point is Marris' distinction between the rate of progress defined as the actual rate of change of productivity and the rate of invention defined as the potential rate of change. (41) The degree to which the two will diverge depends on the gap between techniques of production actually employed at a point in time and the techniques embodying the latest technological advances which could be employed. One of the main factors determining the size of this gap is the rate of replacement. There are two kinds of replacement investment—like for like where savings are primarily due to the cessation of operating inadequacies caused by physical wear and tear, and obsolescent replacements where savings are the result of technical change. Of the two considerations, obsolescence seems to play by far the more important role in replacement decisions. (37) A rapid rate of replacement is also conducive to increasing productivity since it lowers the average age of the capital stock and injects capital embodying the latest improvements in technology.

Marris argues that the rate of invention is determined by the rate of replacement on the strength of the relationship between the rate of replacement and the absolute size of the capital goods market. The larger the absolute size of the latter, he contends, the larger either the number of organisations or the average size of a fixed number. And if inventions occur at random the larger either the number or the average size of producing organisations, the larger the number of inventions.

A second argument for relating the rate of invention to the absolute size of the capital goods market relies on the association of the size of the capital sector with opportunities for vertical disintegration and specialisation. This association was outlined in 3·3. As specialisation occurs dynamic external economies are created, and improvements in either the productive capacity or the productivity of producing new equipment increases the rate of obsolescence of existing equipment. Indeed, this argument implies that the rate of technical progress is in fact a function of the rate of capital accumulation since the absolute size of the capital sector depends on what the rate of growth of capital has been and is now.

A second determinant of the rate of technological progress is the rate of innovation which is closely allied to R&D expenditure. Most important is the type of R&D which induces high levels of technical advance. Describing technological progress, Salter writes that 'continuous disturbance and slow adjustment are essential features. . . Both are continuous processes in time and give rise to a stream of new techniques, each following the other in quick succession. The "once-over" analyses of comparative statistics is only appropriate to changes in technique which are sufficiently great to displace completely all pre-existing methods before they themselves are displaced. It hardly needs to be stressed that such cases are rare; in fact, many experienced observers note that the cumulative effect of small unnoticed modifications and improvements are equally as great as the more significant changes normally regarded as innovations'. (33) Usher argues that 'technological change must be understood as a continuous process of cumulative synthesis emerging out of a perception of deficiencies in existing techniques and knowledge. . . the history of technology can be much more adequately represented from the point of view of continuously emerging novelty than from the romantic concept of occasional innovation at widely spaced intervals'. (42) The thesis that existing technology begets new technology is widely supported. For example, Kaplan comments that 'innovation usually emerges as a logical development of the innovators' established process or product, either because of technological similarities that carry over from the old to the new or because of the necessity of making use of by-products' (43), while to J. M. Clarke innovation 'serves as a point of departure for further innovations that follow'; so and so 'given a problem an idea for its solution may come with the flash of genius mentioned by Schumpeter: but there is more evidence of the kind of genius consisting of technical competence plus persistent work on the succession of problems of which the original problem turns out to be composed'. (44) Penrose also argues that 'even if the primary purpose is to develop ways of reducing the costs and improving the quality of existing products, the exploration and research involved will certainly speed up the production of new knowledge and the creation of new production services within the firm'. (45)

And the fact is that research has become increasingly technically orientated, (46, 47, 48) is carried out for the most part in mammoth corporate enterprises and is increasingly concentrated in industries such as aircraft, electronics, oil-refining, engineering, petro-chemicals and chemicals. Moreover, it is these 'new' industries, spawned by R&D, which are the mainstay of advancing productivity in developed economies. In the U. K., for example, between 1924 and 1950, ten industries contributed the bulk of the increase in output although none of these ten ranked as important in 1924. Having their origin in the scientific and technical discoveries of this century the 'new' industries are heavily capital-intensive, closely related to science and dependent for growth on continual scientific breakthroughs.

A third factor closely related to the rate of technical change is the level of economic interrelatedness. An innovation in one industry induces technical advances in others by creating the dynamic external economies described in 1·10 and 3·3. These economies extend the range of production possibilities in these industries and make possible the application of techniques which were not hitherto economically feasible. But it is also important to recognise that the level of inter-industry linkages is determined to some extent by the level of technology. For different levels of technology permit the establishment of different minimum economic plant sizes so that an increase in vertical disintegration in response, say, to a changing level of demand can occur only if the prevalent technology permits economically feasible plant sizes. And finally, the economies of specialisation which are a by-product of producer interdependence also induce technological progress first because increasing familiarity with a narrow range of products creates the environment for change through the 'learning by doing' process and second, because the resource foundation for research is fostered through the accumulation of know-how in special fields.

What, then, may be inferred about technological levels in Ireland given the framework just described? She lacks a capital goods sector, and therefore industries using and creating advanced technologies while domestic expenditure on R&D is at an extremely low level. (49) However, she does import her capital requirements and since changes in technology will become embodied in such imports, she can gain to some extent from technical advances originating abroad. Insofar as this occurs, the growth of technology is an exogenous variable. A similar argument may be advanced in regard to material inputs. Since the food industries rely almost exclusively on domestic raw materials improvements in quality, variety etc. may only arise due to developments in their sector of origin—domestic agriculture. Industries other than food using imported raw materials or semi-manufactures are in a position to benefit from technological advances abroad affecting techniques of production and the quality, variety and composition of materials. Since such developments are occurring primarily in the rapidly expanding technology oriented industries the gains from technical change should accrue to those industries which are their counterparts in Ireland, and which should, accordingly enjoy the most rapid growth.

This thesis may be tested by examining the growth patterns of industries in developed countries, and the growth patterns of comparable industries in Ireland. Information on the former is taken from the U.N. World Economic Survey (1961), and presented in rank order in Table 6·5 which also contains similar information for Ireland. The U.N. committee, when examining the data for the developed countries, observed that 'the striking similarity in the relative rates of growth of various branches of manufacturing in the developed countries suggests

TABLE 6·5

Rank movements of industry growth rates in Ireland between 1953 &1963 & in some developed economies 1950–1960

Industry	Ireland	UK	USA	Japan	Germany	Italy	France	Australia
Food	10	5	7	9	6	7	7	7
Textiles	4	9	9	7	9	9	8	6
Clothing & footwear	8	8	4	8	3	6	9	8
Wood & furniture	9	7	8	10	8	5	6	9
Paper	3	2	3	4	4	4	4	2
Printing & publications	7	2	4	5	4	—	2	5
Leather prod.	5	10	10	3	10	8	10	—
Chemicals	2	1	1	2	2	1	1	1
Non-Metallic mineral prod.	5	6	6	6	4	2	5	4
Metal & Eng. products	1	2	2	1	1	3	2	3
Rank correlations between sectoral growth patterns in Ireland and		$r=$ +0·34 $r°=$ +0·48	$r=$ +0·47 $r°=$ +0·62	$r=$ +0·87 $r°=$ +0·92	$r=$ +0·29 $r°=$ +0·41	$r=$ +0·48 $r°=$ +0·57	$r=$ +0·47 $r°=$ +0·60	$r=$ +0·62 $r°=$ +0·85

$r°$–leather goods excluded

For ten observations $r=0·63$ is significant at the 5% confidence level.

For nine observations $r=0·67$ is significant at the 5% confidence level.

the existence of common influences. One such influence is technical progress. There is direct evidence that the fast growing industries such as the chemical and engineering industries have been particularly affected by technological advances. It is common knowledge that many firms in these industries derive a high proportion of their sales from processes and products that had not existed prior to the 1950s. While technical progress has also occurred in other industries, its effects have been less far reaching'.

Looking now at the related experience of Ireland, the engineering and chemical industries do indeed rank first and second in growth. Moreover, the rank correlations in Table 6·5 suggest that there has been a tendency for the industry groups which grew most rapidly in developed countries to grow most rapidly in Ireland. For example, discounting leather products as an extreme observation, there is a correlation of +0·48 between the relative growth rates of industry sectors in Ireland and the U.K., of +0·62 for Ireland and the U.S., of +0·92 for Ireland and Japan, of +0·41 for Ireland and Germany, of +0·57 for Ireland and Italy, and of +0·62 for Ireland and France.

It appears, therefore, that the benefits of the technological advances which account for the rapid growth of certain industries in developed economies are diffused in a manner which enables similar sectoral growth patterns in less developed economies. Accordingly, while an explanation of inter-industry relations in the U.K., or in any developed country, may be stated in terms of the interaction of factor substitution, economies of scale and the uneven impact of technical change, an explanation along similar lines of inter-industry relations among industries other than food in Ireland must acknowledge that the third factor is the uneven impact of borrowed technology.

6.5 Conclusion

This chapter started out by selecting three factors—factor substitution, economies of scale and technical advance as possible causes of the pattern of inter-industry relations. Using these three factors as a framework the behaviour of the food industries was examined, and it appeared that the associations between relative movements of different variables could be explained solely in terms of variations among these industries in the elasticity of substitution of capital for labour. However, the case of industries other than food was more complex. While factor substitution may have occurred its effects have been obscured by the impact of the other two factors. The empirical data is consistent with the thesis that the rapid growth industries enjoyed economies of scale, and hence the relative reductions in unit labour and capital costs. It is also consistent with the thesis that the uneven impact of technology is at the root of uneven movements of output, costs and productivity.

It would seem therefore that the interaction of both factors has stimulated the pattern of observed relations. But it is important to recognise that technical advances, so far as industries in Ireland are concerned, are primarily dependent on the technical advances which have either occurred or are occurring in the more highly complex comparable industries in developed countries.

7 PATTERNS OF PRODUCTIVITY INTER-RELATIONSHIPS

7.1 Introduction

Except for the associations between location, plant size and capital intensity, the variables examined on an empirical basis in preceding chapters have in general been treated as separate and unrelated entities. This concluding chapter will draw together these disparate strands and summarise the findings. An analysis will be made of the relationships which exist between the productivity and cost behaviour of an industry and (a) its degree of localisation, (b) its prevalent plant size, (c) its level of capital intensity and (d), its level of concentration and competitiveness. Such an analysis will give an overall view of the way in which certain facets of an industry's structural organisation have been related to the industry's performance over time, and may also throw some light on issues such as whether certain locational patterns discourage industry growth, whether the prevalence of monopoly and oligopoly leads to poor performance and consumer exploitation and whether high capital intensive industries have a greater capacity for growth than less capital intensive industries.

7.2 Other productivity inter-relationships

Table 7·1 presents the output, cost, productivity etc. movements of industries in specified localisation groupings. Looking at relative growth rates it seems clear that industry location pattern has not been a factor affecting industry growth. Although industries with below average rates of expansion were either very highly localised (C.O.L. > 0·60) or dispersed (C.O.L. < 0·40), it would be wrong to read any significance into these results. Indeed, on the basis of just two categories of localisation there is no difference between the rates of expansion achieved by industries in the medium and low localisation

TABLE 7·1

Output & cost movements in industries grouped according to level of localisation

	All industries	0–0·29	0·30–0·39	0·40–0·44	0·45–0·49	0·50–0·59	0·60–over	0–0·39	0·40–0·49	0–0·49	0·50–over
Volume output	150	138	136	164	163	163	136	137	164	150	150
Employment	112	97	115	112	118	124	119	100	117	108	122
Output per head	134	142	118	146	138	131	114	137	140	139	123
Operatives	111	97	114	110	116	123	117	99	115	107	120
Output per operative	135	142	119	149	141	133	116	138	143	140	125
Earnings per operative	167	162	168	165	171	170	170	163	170	164	170
Unit wage cost	124	114	141	111	121	128	147	118	118	117	136
Salary earners	121	100	119	127	129	137	130	104	128	116	133
Unit salary cost	135	133	136	122	133	134	149	133	129	133	140
Unit labour cost	125	116	139	113	124	129	147	120	120	120	137
Unit gross margin cost	131	130	154	101	130	134	133	138	120	129	135
Unit material cost	104	123	91	94	91	132	102	107	92	99	111
Gross Prices	111	122	101	96	101	132	110	114	99	107	118

group (C.O.L. <0·50) and by those with high localisation
(C.O.L.>0·50). Relative price movements of industries within
localisation groupings follow an expected pattern—in each
case they are clearly related to relative movements of unit
material costs. Earnings per operative were higher in the more
highly localised industries and presumably reflect the tendency
for wage differentials to exist between highly urbanised and
less urbanised areas and the higher costs of living in the former.
Of most interest, however, is the behaviour of costs and labour
productivity. While the highly localised industries accounted
for the bulk of the increase in employment, they secured the
smallest advances in labour productivity coupled with the
largest increases in all components of cost and in prices. In
contrast, with the exception of industries with C.O.L.'s between
0·30 and 0·39 the average increase in labour productivity among
industries in each other category was above the national
average.

In Table 7·2 industry cost and output movements are organised on the basis of prevalent industry plant sizes—industries
for which no prevalent plant sizes are available being omitted
from the analysis. The results are not what might have been
expected. Industries in the large and largish plant size category
have had growth rates well below the national average. And
although the bias to large plant industries recorded the largest
increases in output and labour productivity, large plant industries as a single group still rank behind both small and
medium plant industries with respect to growth of output and
labour productivity. In fact on almost every criterion of performance large plant industries make the poorest showing,
having the largest increases in unit labour cost, unit gross
margin cost, unit material cost and gross prices.

Accordingly, to the extent that large plant sizes reflect
larger scales of production, it may be inferred that industries in
which production was organised on a relatively large scale
have made the least contribution to the growth of output and
productivity between 1953 and 1963. Indeed, the major proportion of the increases may be attributed to industries characterised by smallish or moderate scales of production. There
is no reason to believe therefore that large scale organisation is

TABLE 7·2

Output & Cost movements in industries grouped according to their prevalent size of plant

	average	small	smallish	bias to small	medium	bias to large	largish	large	small[a]	small & medium	large[b]
Volume output	152	140	205	169	159	253	124	127	154	155	149
Employment	114	95	135	122	111	162	125	104	107	108	125
Output per head	133	147	152	139	143	156	99	122	144	144	119
Operatives	112	95	133	120	108	161	124	103	106	107	124
Output per operative	136	147	154	141	147	157	100	123	145	145	120
Earnings per operative	167	159	173	172	171	158	169	173	161	166	168
Unit wage cost	123	108	112	122	116	101	169	141	111	114	173
Salary earners	123	99	145	131	136	170	132	115	114	118	144
Unit salary cost	133	123	123	126	132	104	166	155	127	—	136
Unit labour cost	124	110	115	123	119	101	169	143	114	115	137
Unit gross margin cost	132	116	129	147	123	133	130	148	132	130	133
Unit material cost	102	107	113	92	94	114	114	110	101	99	105
Gross Prices	109	109	117	103	104	114	120	120	106	106	113

(a) Includes small, smallish and bias to small.
(b) Includes bias to large, largish and large.

per se a prerequisite for a high rate of expansion and productivity growth; the evidence in fact points to the opposite conclusion.

Turning now to Table 7·3 it appears that the classification of industry cost and output performance on the basis of industry

TABLE 7·3

Output & cost movements in industries grouped according to level of capital intensity

	all indus-tries	0–1·50	1·60–3·00	3·10–6·00	6·10 over	0–3·00	3·10 over
Volume output	150	158	148	163	129	153	146
Employment	116	113	118	129	109	115	119
Output per head	129	140	125	126	118	133	123
Operatives	115	112	116	127	106	113	117
Output per operative	130	141	128	128	122	135	125
Earnings per operative	168	166	166	172	167	167	170
Unit wage cost	129	118	130	134	137	124	136
Salary earners	126	123	130	136	117	126	126
Unit salary cost	137	127	141	145	140	135	141
Unit labour cost	131	120	133	136	138	125	138
Unit gross margin cost	132	142	121	136	133	131	135
Unit material cost	103	121	98	121	99	105	101
Gross prices	111	123	105	127	105	112	110

levels of relative capital intensity reveals little in the way of significant trends. In broadest terms industries of relatively low capital intensity (h.p. per operative < 3·0) have recorded below average increases in cost and above average increases in labour productivity and output. The high capital intensive industries (h.p. per operative > 6·00) have been the least expansionary with the smallest increases in output, labour productivity and employment. At the same time they achieved an absolute reduction in unit material cost and a below average increase in prices.

However, it has been noted that horse-power per operative as a measure of capital intensity is biased in favour of industries using bulky or heavy raw materials and that it may primarily reflect the weight of such materials.[1] Accordingly, it could be argued that analysis of industries with horse-power indexes below 6·00 would provide a more meaningful indication of how mechanisation in actual manufacturing processes. i.e., as a substitution of capital for labour, has affected industry performance. But even on this basis no clear-cut pattern emerges. For, while it would make the most capital intensive industries (h.p. index 3·10—6·00) the most expansionary, these industries would also have incurred below average increases in labour productivity and above average increases in all elements of cost and prices. The least capital intensive industries (h.p. indexes 1·50 or less) would still have secured the largest increase in labour productivity and reduction in labour cost, and an output expansion considerably higher than that achieved by the medium capital intensive industries. Accordingly, while bearing in mind the many inadequacies of the horse-power measure, it seems reasonable to suggest that inter-industry variations in levels of capital intensity are unrelated to inter-industry variations in productivity and output growth— low capital intensive industries have in no way been at a disadvantage *vis-à-vis* high capital intensive industries. What is important, of course, where growth and productivity are concerned, is not the absolute level of capital stocks but relative rates of growth.

The final question to be considered in this section is whether any relation exists between the level of industry concentration and market performance. Table 7·4 presents three sets of data pertinent to this issue all of which show beyond doubt that the high concentration industries have recorded the worst performance in every aspect of output, cost, price and productivity change. The disparities in performance are more easily appreciated when industries are considered on the basis of their competitive levels. Those approaching perfect competition have been the most expansionary. They also have had the largest increases in labour productivity and employment, the

---

[1]Cf. O'Malley (3) Table 3, Chapter 4, page 6. Nine of the industries with h.p. per operative greater than 6·00 are also the nine with the highest weight of material per head.

TABLE 7·4

Output & cost movements in industries grouped according to level of concentration & competition

	concentration 1954(a)				concentration 1964 & competitive levels						
	all indus-tries	high	medium	low	all indus-tries	high	medium	low	(b)	(c)	(d)
Volume output	153	130	161	157	150	119	167	156	119	147	175
Employment	117	109	122	113	116	106	121	117	106	116	122
Output per head	131	119	132	139	129	112	138	133	112	127	143
Operatives	115	107	120	112	119	104	119	116	104	116	119
Output per operative	133	121	134	140	130	114	140	134	114	127	147
Earnings per operative	168	169	167	170	168	170	170	166	170	168	169
Unit wage cost	126	140	125	121	129	149	121	124	149	132	115
Salary earners	126	123	136	116	126	118	133	122	118	118	139
Unit salary cost	135	153	136	125	137	162	127	129	162	132	126
Unit labour cost	128	142	127	122	131	152	123	125	152	133	118
Unit gross margin cost	132	162	129	120	132	166	129	111	166	139	111
Unit material cost	104	115	103	97	103	111	113	91	111	120	89
Gross prices	110	125	109	104	110	124	117	97	124	125	95

(a) Structural clay products & sugar, cocoa, chocolate & sugar confectionery have been omitted since separate data for their components were not available.
(b) Tendency to monoply.
(c) Tendency to oligopoly.
(d) Tendency to perfect competition.

smallest increases in all elements of cost and have realised an absolute reduction in their price levels. On the other hand, the performance of industries with monopoly characteristics provides a striking contrast: the lowest rate of expansion, the smallest increases in labour productivity and employment, the largest increases in labour and gross margin costs and substantial price increases. Indeed, the very large increases in unit gross margin cost coupled with the slow growth of output and labour productivity may indicate that factor substitution was relatively inelastic and that opportunities for realising economies of scale were almost negligible. However, since unit gross margin cost may also be regarded as an indicator of profit, the large increases in both unit gross margins and prices could reflect higher profit margins. The considerably below average increases in unit margin costs in the most competitive industries may indicate, in addition to the impact of scale economies, a relative fall of profit margins due to the pressures of competition.

7.3 Factors determining the pattern of inter-relations

The picture which emerges from the preceding analysis raises the question: why have the highly localised, large plant, high concentration industries had the smallest increases in output and productivity and above average increases in all elements of costs and prices? It must be recognised, of course, that given any one of the above relations, say, for example, the association of high localisation and poor market performance the other two would be likely to occur since the analyses of Chapters 3 and 4 revealed strong associations between levels of localisation and plant size, plant size and levels of concentration and levels of concentration and levels of localisation.

It is tempting to pick on the most obvious explanation and to ascribe the high cost and low output orientation to the vices of monopolistic competition and relatively high growth and declining costs to the virtues of perfect competition. However, while an explanation along these lines is plausible and indeed may be true to some extent, it is nevertheless far too unqualified to withstand rigorous criticism, and will for the moment be rejected. A second, and it will be argued, more meaningful,

9

explanation can be drawn up using as a framework the explicit variables affecting the growth of productivity (factor substitution, economies of scale, technical change) and their inter-relationships with the cycles of industry growth.

A quick review of some previously established findings will provide the desired perspective. Given that factors such as the nature of an industry's technical processes, products or materials determine its location pattern; that prevalent plant size is then a reflection of the scale of production economically feasible within the ambit of locational constraints; that large plant sizes are a rational economic structure in some industries; that the markets of large plant industries in general are smaller than those of other industries; that markets in Ireland are small no matter what criterion is employed, it follows that absolute size of large plant industry markets is indeed very small, and that efficient production can be achieved only if the competing units are also few in number. The prevalence of high concentration in these industries is therefore to be expected.

Moreover, the monopoly oriented industries are characterised by two other features which are at the root of their poor market performance. A very high proportion are either 'old' in terms of industry life cycles or are producing products for which demand is income inelastic. Foremost among the 'old' industries are railroad equipment and ship building which have, to a large extent, been rendered technologically obsolete, and glass and fertilisers which rely on capital intensive products of slow technological progress; while industries producing income inelastic products include butter blending, distilling, brewing, sugar, brushes, brooms and tobacco. (53, 54) Thus over two-thirds of the monopoly oriented industries are at a stage in their life cycles when markets are contracting, static or slowly expanding due to the levelling off of consumer demand, the slow growth of industries using their products or the availability of substitute products. Indeed, although no association was found between relative rates of industry growth and concentration it is reasonable to argue that high concentration is as much a possible effect of relatively slow growth as a cause of it since less efficient units in slow growth industries are invariably forced out of business.

The fact, then, that the high monopoly oriented industries have had below average increases in productivity and above average increases in costs and prices merely re-affirms the pattern of relationships observed for the relative movements of these variables in Chapter 5. Being characteristically 'old', monopoly oriented industries encountered a slow rate of technological advance. Collectively they were faced with at best slowly expanding markets. Not only were the opportunities for realising economies of scale limited but attempts to increase labour productivity through capital substitution were unlikely to yield significant cost savings. Moreover, since relatively low rates of technical change were embodied in new capital equipment decisions either to add to or replace the capital stock were also unlikely to yield benefits commensurate with the returns to similar decisions in more technologically progressive industries.

Indeed, industries which are highly capitalised may have relatively low rates of capital formation. For example, this may happen when an industry is capitalised to the extent that opportunities for achieving further technical economies through continued factor substitution are exhausted. Further increases in labour productivity becomes primarily dependent on the element of technical progress embodied in replacements to the capital stock rather than in net additions to it. And the prospect for any sizeable increases in productivity are poor if the industry is also operating in virtually stagnant markets and the available technology has a slow rate of improvement.

As regards the explanation that varying types of market structures have been the key determinant of market performance, it is doubtful whether the above average output and productivity cost record of industries classified as highly competitive can be ascribed to the actual rigours of competition. In the first place, the Irish market had the benefit of a very high level of protection during the decade. Second, the classification contains three separate industry components in which the intensity of competition varied considerably and which recorded diverse movements of costs and output. (Table 7·5) The industries approximating most closely to perfect competition were no more than average performers in terms of output

TABLE 7·5

Output & cost movements in sub-categories of the industries classified as most competitive

	industries with low concentration, small plants, small size ratios & many units (A)	industries with low concentration, small size ratios & many units (B)	A + B	industries with medium concentration, small size ratios & many units	Average for all industries
Volume output	152	137	146	209	150
Employment	112	120	114	130	116
Output per head	136	114	128	161	129
Operatives	111	119	113	125	115
Output per operative	137	115	129	167	130
Earnings per operative	165	163	165	174	168
Unit wage cost	120	142	128	104	129
Salary earners	117	130	120	167	126
Unit salary cost	126	150	134	122	137
Unit labour cost	122	143	129	108	131
Unit gross margin cost	114	93	108	116	132
Unit material cost	97	89	93	103	103
Gross prices	101	93	98	106	110

expansion and productivity growth, the dynamic element in market performance being provided by industries with medium concentration, small plant size ratios and many units, conditions which make impossible any rigid conclusion regarding the influence of level of competition. On the other hand, at least five of the nineteen industries deemed highly competitive (the three clothing industries, shirtmaking and furniture) manufacture products for which demand is income elastic, a further three (chemicals and drugs, machinery except electrical, and electrical machinery) are relatively young in terms of industry life cycles while only three (bacon, dairy products and malting), appear to be definitely in the category of income inelastic demand. (53, 54) Accordingly, although the conclusion is subject to all of the usual qualifications, it does appear likely that the rapid growth of industries classified as competitive has been due more to their comparative youth in terms of industry life cycles and to a prevalence of high income elasticities of demand, both of which provide the opportunities to avail of more progressive technologies and economies of scale, than to the stimuli of competition.

7.4 Conclusion

This chapter examined the relationships between industry market performance and certain structural variables, and found (a) that location structure has not been a factor affecting industry growth rates etc.; (b) that industries organised on a relatively small scale basis have had for the most part more rapid growth rates and superior market performances in terms of productivity, costs and prices than large scale industries; (c) that inter-industry variations in relative capital intensity have had no discernible affect on any aspect of industry performance and (d), that the highly competitive industries have had strikingly better market records than either oligopolistic or monopolistic industries. Indeed, monopolistic industries finished a poor third on almost every count of market behaviour.

The absence of an association between industry location structures and industry growth rates etc. does not imply that a specific industry's growth potential is unrelated to its location pattern. On the contrary, the two are closely related as may be inferred from Chapter 1 where factors such as the nature of technical processes, products and raw materials were isolated as the main determinants of location patterns. Indeed the present finding bears out the argument of that chapter that the location organisation of industry has an inherent logic of its own. For if industries tend to follow the location pattern which facilitates efficient operation there is no reason why inter-industry variations in localisation should be related to inter-industry variations in market performance. Similarly, if regional development programmes are to prove successful in combating the present imbalance of industrial employment it is not sufficient that they provide the climate and incentives which foster the growth of poles of development. Of crucial importance is the need to preserve the logic of location structures. In other words, regional programmes must ensure that the regional location of new enterprises conforms to the location characteristics of the units in question .

The fact that small plant industries achieved a market performance superior to that of large scale industries suggests that the frequent assertion that more rapid growth can be achieved by the promotion of large scale enterprises may be misleading. Proponents of the large-scale thesis fail to distinguish between (a) an industry's growth prospects and (b) the technical (in the narrowest sense) and physical nature of the activities it carries out and products manufactured. The former depend on income elasticities of demand, degree of R&D orientation, capacity for technological progress etc., while the latter determines feasible scales of production units. There is no *a priori* reason why a growth industry should have large scale characteristics nor is there any inherent link between growth potential and scale of organisation. Indeed, relatively small scale units were typical of the faster growing sectors in Ireland during the fifties and early sixties. The implications for industry development policies are clear. As long as these policies foster the development of growth industries the question of whether or not production is organised on a large scale becomes largely irrelevant.

In conclusion, two aspects of the inter-industry analysis of Chapter 6 are worth pursuing. The first concerns the absence of any significant association between movements in earnings per operative and output per operative. Now, one of the most frequently cited obstacles to economic growth is a round of wages increases in excess of the growth of productivity. The resulting rise in costs is passed on to prices, rising prices encourage a further round of wage demands which in turn raise costs and prices, and in this way the familiar wage price spiral takes hold. The consequences are reduced competitiveness, loss of markets, a decline in exports, and a possible rise in unemployment. In addition inflation increases social inequities because of a redistribution of income away from those living on fixed incomes, the poor, the elderly and in general the underprivileged members of society.

There are strong grounds, therefore, for adopting some form

of incomes policy, the more controversial question being, of course, what kind. While this is not the place to discuss the many and varied proposals which have been advocated or implemented, at one time or another, there is one aspect of the issue which may be fruitfully discussed here. It has been argued that each industry's wage structure should be related in some way to its capacity to increase productivity. In other words, industries with above average productivity increases would incur above average increases in wages while industries with below average advances in productivity would incur below average wage increases. Thus, it is argued, not only would workers have an incentive to increase productivity but a structure of inter-industry wage differentials would tend to increase the mobility of labour and redirect employment to industries in which productivity is rapidly advancing. But, apart from considerations of the social inequities which could follow, such a programme may be criticised for its economic implications. It amounts to an indirect subsidy of low productivity achieving industries and could lead to a reduction in the overall rate of productivity growth. Industries with a slow advance in productivity would no longer incur above average increases in unit labour costs while the distribution of all or most of the gains from the increase in productivity of the rapid growth industries would leave little room for reductions in unit labour cost. Consequently, there would be a vastly reduced tendency for low productivity growth industries to incur above average increases in relative prices and for high productivity achieving industries to achieve below average increases in relative prices. As a result, the structure of demand would tend to fossilise, growth as a process of movements through a hierarchy of goods would become both slower and distorted, industries with rapid growth characteristics would expand at rates below their potential while declining industries would receive a measure of protection from the rigours of competition.

It seems clear therefore, that an effective incomes policy must incorporate the principle that similar wage structures should prevail in industries employing similar types of labour, thereby ensuring that inter-industry movements of productivity and wages are unrelated. If this is so, movements in unit labour costs and productivity will be inversely related. Should artificial support of an industry become desirable (for example, if the expanding sectors are unable to absorb the labour released from declining sectors) then specific support measures may be introduced. But even here support must be regarded as a temporary stop-gap measure. In the longer term, frictions and imperfections in the labour market should be alleviated by vigorous manpower policies relating to training and retraining, placement, vocational and geographical mobility and measures designed to eliminate the social costs and hardships which frequently accompany redundancy.

One final point which should be emphasised is the pivotal position of the price mechanism in the growth process. For it may be recalled that the rapidity of growth, when viewed as a sequence of movements through a hierarchy of goods, depends, among other things, on the relations between movements of output, productivity, costs and prices. If above average increases in output are associated with below average increases in all elements of costs and prices, then the process of movement and hence the rate of growth are speeded up. In Ireland, the absence of a relation between differential movements of output and prices caused by the exogenous nature of the price component of unit material cost interferes with the movement process and may retard growth, at least to some extent. Unfortunately, this problem has no immediate solution. Ultimately, its impact may be reduced through import substitution but the possibility of this occurring on a large scale, in the foreseeable future at least, is remote.

APPENDIX

Industry location quotients

	Jams, jellies, canned & preserved fruit & vegetables	Cocoa, chocolate & sugar confectionery products	Canned preserved meat & other meat products	Bacon curing, sausages & pig-meat products	Dairy Products	Sugar
Leinster	1·93	1·83	1·48	0·52	0·46	0·81
Carlow	a	a	a	0·59	0·17	27·30
Dublin Co. Bor.	3·82	3·37	1·71	0·45	0·44	0·10
Dunlaoire	0·56b	1·19	0·45b	0·15b	—	a
Dublin County	1·68	2·89	1·12	0·24	0·63	0·12
Total Dublin	3·25	3·15	1·54	0·46	0·45	0·11
Kildare	1·73	0·68	10·45	a	a	0·51
Kilkenny	—	0·27	a	2·33	2·34	0·25
Laois	0·56b	a	a	0·95	0·88	1·74
Longford	—	0·18	1·24	a	a	—
Louth	a	a	a	0·42	a	—
Meath	a	0·34	1·90	a	0·23	—
Offaly	a	—	0·41	1·14	0·10	—
Westmeath	a	a	a	a	0·36	—
Wexford	0·29b	a	a	1·30	0·50	—
Wicklow	a	0·60	a	a	0·22	—
Munster	0·15	0·37	0·97	1·93	2·36	1·54
Clare	—	a	—	a	1·11	a
Cork Co. Bor.	0·84	0·71	a	4·37	0·60	a
Cork County	0·08b	0·34	0·11b	0·36	3·09	2·67
Total Cork	0·15	0·42	0·13	1·30	2·51	—
Kerry	a	0·46	—	1·60	1·77	a
Limerick Co. Bor.	a	1·32	0·86	8·12	2·63	—
Limerick County	a	a	1·08	0·19	4·00	a
Total Limerick	a	0·34	1·00	3·11	3·31	a
Tipperary N.R.	—	—	6·15	1·49	1·82	9·38
Tipperary S.R.	—	0·60	4·32	0·77	2·47	1·17
Total Tipperary	—	0·33	5·14	1·08	2·18	4·84
Waterford Bor.	—	0·22b	—	15·29	0·92	a
Waterford County	0·59b	0·14b	0·50b	1·34	2·95	a
Total Waterford	0·38	0·17	0·31	6·74	2·16	a
Connacht	0·10	0·03	0·07b	0·87	0·22	1·03
Galway	a	a	a	0·06b	0·05b	2·61
Leitrim	0·93	—	—	a	0·64	—
Mayo	—	a	a	1·84	0·04b	1·38
Roscommon	—	a	a	0·58	0·08b	—
Sligo	a	0·15	a	1·78	1·01	—
Ulster (part of)	0·32	0·18	a	0·67	0·74	0·07
Cavan	a	a	—	1·53	1·11	—
Donegal	—	0·36	—	0·25	0·25	0·14b
Monaghan	1·29	—	a	0·52	1·37	—

(*a*) Denotes less than 10 persons employed in the industry in the county.
(*b*) Denotes between 10 and 20 persons employed in the industry in the county.

	Bread & flour confectionery	Biscuits	Grain milling & animal feed stuffs	Other food stuffs	Malting	Brewing	Distilling	Soft drinks
Leinster	1·19	2·04	0·87	1·28	1·86	1·86	1·41	1·00
Carlow	0·74	—	2·51	a	7·26	—	—	5·46
Dublin Co. Bor.	1·55	4·03	0·69	2·13	0·64	3·11	2·31	1·32
Dunlaoire	1·00	3·95	0·27	0·85	0·20^b	1·45	1·51	0·64^b
Dublin County	1·07	1·91	0·60	1·53	0·43^b	2·89	1·32	0·46
Total Dublin	1·44	3·66	0·65	1·95	0·58	2·96	2·08	1·13
Kildare	0·86	a	1·29	0·43^b	5·14	0·13^b	a	—
Kilkenny	0·96	—	1·83	a	1·38	1·79	—	0·27^b
Laois	0·45	—	2·30	—	5·26	0·74	—	a
Longford	0·77	a	—	a	—	a	—	a
Louth	1·58	—	1·28	1·34	0·61^b	1·36	0·98	0·57
Meath	0·87	a	0·34	0·62	a	0·10^b	a	0·70
Offaly	0·71	—	1·11	0·42^b	8·42	a	3·57	1·05
Westmeath	0·78	—	0·14^b	a	a	a	a	0·93
Wexford	0·77	a	1·19	a	8·83	0·13^b	a	1·44
Wicklow	0·94	0·52	0·74	0·73	—	0·66	a	a
Munster	1·05	0·07	1·53	0·87	0·37	0·36	1·13	1·22
Clare	0·43	a	0·73	0·37^b	—	—	—	0·20
Cork Co. Bor.	2·54	a	3·56	2·19	a	2·01	6·67	2·20
Cork County	0·93	a	1·42	1·46	0·42	0·34	1·62	0·96
Total Cork	1·31	a	1·92	1·63	0·38	0·73	2·79	1·24
Kerry	0·71	a	0·54	0·16^b	—	a	—	1·09
Lmerick Co. Bor.	1·73	0·64	6·39	0·32^b	—	0·32	a	1·85
Limerick County	0·60	a	0·33	a	—	a	a	1·10
Total Limerick	1·02	0·31	2·82	0·20^b	—	0·15	a	1·03
Tipperary N.R.	0·64	a	0·18^b	a	3·39	—	—	2·40
Tipperary S.R.	0·97	a	1·32	0·29^b	—	a	—	1·72
Total Tipperary	0·82	a	0·81	0·08^b	1·52	a	—	2·02
Waterford Co. Bor.	2·21	—	2·20	0·92^b	—	1·07	—	0·66^b
Waterford County	1·00	—	1·12	1·47^b	—	a	—	0·79
Total Waterford	1·47	—	1·54	1·00	—	0·49	—	0·74
Connacht	0·53	a	0·51	0·65	a	0·05	—	0·78
Galway	0·55	a	0·31	1·45	a	0·06^b	—	1·23
Leitrim	0·49	—	a	—	—	—	—	—
Mayo	0·51	—	0·54	0·21^b	—	a	—	0·62
Roscommon	0·27	—	0·38	0·30^b	—	a	—	a
Sligo	0·88	a	1·45	a	—	0·17^b	—	1·05
Ulster (part of)	4·39	a	0·76	0·52	—	a	—	0·50
Cavan	0·17	—	0·22	0·73	—	a	—	0·76
Donegal	0·79	a	1·11	0·59	—	a	—	0·55
Monaghan	0·45	—	0·63	a	—	—	—	0·52^b

(a) Denotes less than 10 persons employed in the industry in the county.
(b) Denotes between 10 and 20 persons employed in the industry in the county.

	Tobacco	Clothing	Footwear	Shirts	Made up textiles	Hosiery & knitted goods	Woollen & worsted
Leinster	1·97	1·66	1·38	0·90	1·50	1·13	0·98
Carlow	—	0·22	1·25	a	a	—	0·17
Dublin Co. Bor.	2·76	3·07	0·47	1·35	2·18	1·60	0·45
Dunlaoire	4·63	1·03	1·09	3·11	2·45	2·14	0·62
Dublin Co.	2·22	1·26	0·19	1·84	0·63	2·53	1·17
Total Dublin	2·79	2·63	0·46	1·55	—	1·79	0·58
Kildare	—	0·12	0·37	a	b	0·71	0·69
Kilkenny	—	0·12	1·59	a	0·25^b	0·62	0·64
Laois	—	0·18	a	—	—	a	3·10
Longford	—	0·17	a	—	—	a	0·20^b
Louth	7·95	0·18	15·51	a	0·72	0·46	a
Meath	—	0·57	1·66	0·33^b	0·55	0·22	1·75
Offaly	—	0·16	3·73	—	7·92	a	6·10
Westmeath	a	0·14	—	—	0·66	0·59	1·29
Wexford	—	0·18	—	—	a	a	1·78
Wicklow	0·29^b	0·45	a	0·58	0·30^b	0·41	0·21
Munster	0·17	0·50	0·70	0·17	0·85	1·04	1·23
Clare	—	0·18	a	—	0·48	0·58	0·11^b
Cork Co. Bor.	0·53	1·30	2·51	1·57	2·53	6·08	2·27
Cork Co.	0·13	0·48	0·07	0·08^b	0·25	1·03	2·84
Total Cork	0·22	1·11	0·64	0·43	0·78	2·21	2·70
Kerry	a	0·02	1·56	a	—	0·36	0·14
Limerick Co. Bor.	0·89	2·01	1·59	—	2·74	0·54	a
Limerick Co.	a	0·03	0·08^b	a	a	0·12^a	a
Total Limerick	0·39	0·90	0·64	a	0·58	0·28	
Tipperary N.R.	—	0·12	0·09^b	—	—	0·10	0·45
Tipperary S.R.	—	0·30	1·60	a	a	0·09^b	0·83
Total Tipperary	—	0·26	0·93	a	—	0·10	0·19
Waterford Co. Bor.	a	0·18	a	—	8·90	a	—
Waterford Co.	—	0·10	a	—	0·59^b	a	0·38
Total Waterford	—	0·13	a	—	3·81	a	0·15
Connacht	0·06^b	0·31	0·20	0·14	0·13	0·34	0·28
Galway	a	0·39	0·45	—	0·22	0·20	0·19
Leitrim	—	0·14	—	—	—	0·18	—
Mayo	a	0·33	0·11	0·49	a	0·83	0·71
Roscommon	—	0·13	a	—	0·34	a	—
Sligo	a	0·34	a	—	—	a	a
Ulster (part of)	0·11^b	0·25	1·38	6·40	0·23	1·35	1·67
Cavan	—	0·31	1·34	a	0·36	—	0·46
Donegal	0·18^b	0·24	a	12·65	0·26	2·30	3·08
Monaghan	a	0·20	4·41	0·37^b	a	0·84	a

(a) Denotes less than 10 persons employed in the industry in the county.
(b) Denotes between 10 and 20 persons employed in the industry in the county.

	Jute, rayon, nylon, cordage etc.	Linen, cotton & poplin	Furniture & brushes	Wood & Cork	Glass	Clay & cement	Printing & publishing
Leinster	1·14	1·56	1·50	0·88	1·32	1·36	1·68
Carlow	—	—	0·53	0·88	a	1·18	0·27
Dublin Co. Bor.	0·52	0·63	2·26	0·69	1·52	0·75	3·02
Dunlaoire	1·17	0·97	1·04	0·31	0·84	0·47	1·43
Dublin Co.	0·73	1·41	1·07	0·69	1·14	2·19	1·73
Total Dublin	0·60	0·78	1·98	0·66	1·41	0·97	2·70
Kildare	0·94	2·20	0·37	0·88	a	3·35	0·38
Kilkenny	a	—	0·22[b]	1·72	0·50	0·94	0·33
Laois	a	—	0·39	2·04	a	2·33	0·15
Longford	1·35	0·96	0·53	1·51	—	0·68	0·46
Louth	0·21[b]	9·94	1·85	0·70	a	4·59	0·88
Meath	0·21[b]	4·12	4·18	1·49	—	3·45	0·17
Offaly	5·86	a	0·35	0·78	a	0·74	0·15
Westmeath	0·64	7·91	0·22[b]	1·05	a	0·24	0·33
Wexford	—	—	0·28	0·87	0·65	0·79	0·56
Wicklow	1·90	—	0·20	1·15	11·04	0·43	0·88
Munster	1·47	0·30	0·56	1·24	1·13	0·86	0·52
Clare	4·56	—	a	1·95	—	0·85	0·13
Cork Co. Bor.	1·57	a	2·18	0·78	0·40	0·56	2·19
Cork. Co.	1·06	0·70	0·47	1·20	0·91	0·51	0·33
Total Cork	1·18	0·55	0·87	1·10	0·79	0·52	0·77
Kerry	a	—	a	1·56	a	0·25	0·31
Limerick Co. Bor.	0·44	—	1·55	0·58	—	2·90	0·95
Limerick Co.	a	—	0·21	1·06	—	3·03	0·04[b]
Total Limerick	0·18	—	0·71	0·88	—	2·98	0·38
Tipperary N.R.	a	0·94	0·12[b]	1·53	1·88	0·27	0·23
Tipperay S.R.	a	—	0·20[b]	1·74	a	0·08	0·32
Total Tipperary	a	0·42	0·16	1·65	0·90	0·16	0·28
Waterford Co. Bor.	14·78	—	1·77	0·20[a]	18·71	0·28	1·75
Waterford Co.	1·03	0·32	0·40	0·74	1·20	0·21	0·19
Total Waterford	6·35	0·20	0·93	0·53	7·99	0·24	0·79
Connacht	0·11	1·08	0·32	0·82	0·23	0·32	0·21
Galway	0·18	1·19	0·46	0·83	0·59	0·31	0·25
Leitrim	—	—	—	0·66	—	0·04	0·08[b]
Mayo	—	0·70	0·31	0·66	a	0·37	0·15
Roscommon	—	0·82	0·11[b]	0·48	—	0·42	0·17
Sligo	—	2·65	0·35	1·73	a	0·29	0·32
Ulster (part of)	0·11	0·52[b]	0·94	1·20	0·09	0·87	0·19
Cavan	0·24[b]	—	0·03	1·27	—	1·58	0·20
Donegal	—	0·10[b]	0·09[b]	1·18	0·19	0·34	0·21
Monaghan	—	—	3·55	1·16	—	1·18	0·15

(a) Denotes less than 10 persons employed in the industry in the county.
(b) Denotes between 10 and 20 persons employed in the industry in the county.

	Paper & paper products	Fertilisers	Soaps & candles	Pharmaceutical preparations, drugs & medicines	Paints, vegetable & marine oils & other chemical products
Leinster	1·77	1·34	1·91	1·66	1·61
Carlow	a	—	a	a	a
Dublin Co. Bor.	2·23	1·75	3·74	2·57	2·38
Dunlaoire	0·62	0·52^b	2·98	3·49	1·41
Dublin Co.	5·50	0·54	1·79	3·17	2·32
Total Dublin	2·68	1·47	3·36	2·73	2·31
Kildare	3·23	—	—	a	0·23^b
Kilkenny	0·10	1·34	—	a	a
Laois	0·28^b	—	a	a	a
Longford	—	—	a	—	a
Louth	a	2·40	a	1·10	4·32
Meath	0·39	a	a	a	0·28^b
Offaly	—	0·53^a	a	1·08	a
Westmeath	—	—	a	a	a
Wexford	—	1·57	—	—	a
Wicklow	1·52	5·23	a	0·54^b	1·93
Munster	0·51	1·03	0·30	0·59	0·55
Clare	0·69	—	—	a	a
Cork Co. Bor.	0·92	5·11	2·11	0·48	3·06
Cork Co.	0·07	0·79	0·02^b	0·28	0·66
Total Cork	0·27	1·79	0·51	0·33	1·22
Kerry	0·08^b	—	a	a	—
Limerick Co. Bor.	a	a	a	1·50	0·44^b
Limerick Co.	0·17^b	2·14	—	a	a
Total Limerick	0·12	1·42	a	0·55	0·16
Tipperary N.R.	0·39	—	a	5·34	—
Tipperary S.R.	a	0·22^b	a	—	a
Total Tipperary	0·21	0·13	a	2·89	a
Waterford Co. Bor.	7·52	2·37	a	a	0·89
Waterford Co.	0·65	a	a	a	a
Total Waterford	3·30	1·03	a	a	0·34
Connacht	a	0·27	a	1·93	0·27
Galway	a	0·18^b	a	0·12^b	0·53
Leitrim	a	—	a	—	a
Mayo	a	0·13^a	a	0·43	0·21
Roscommon	a	—	—	a	a
Sligo	a	1·34	a	a	a
Ulster (part of)	0·08	0·25	a	0·08^b	0·39
Cavan	—	—	a	—	0·31^b
Donegal	0·16	0·50	a	a	0·59
Monaghan	—	—	—	a	a

(a) Denotes less than 10 persons employed in the industry in the county.
(b) Denotes between 10 and 20 persons employed in the industry in the county.

	Machinery except electrical	Electrical machinery & appliances	Ship building	Rail loco-motives	Assembly of mechanical vehicles	Metal products	Other vehicles
Leinster	1·63	1·91	0·87	1·68	1·65	1·20	1·78
Carlow	0·43	—	—	—	—	2·72	—
Dublin Co. Bor.	1·80	2·81	1·60	3·36	2·98	1·77	3·49
Dunlaoire	1·06	1·60	1·53	a	1·21	0·65	0·77^b
Dublin Co.	2·30	3·40	0·45	2·41	0·21	0·81	2·44
Total Dublin	1·84	2·83	1·40	3·00	2·72	1·54	3·11
Kildare	0·21	a	—	—	0·12^b	1·65	a
Kilkenny	1·28	0·17^b	—	—	0·10^b	0·36	a
Laois	0·31	a	a	—	—	0·75	a
Longford	—	—	—	—	—	0·23	a
Louth	4·88	3·65	0·51^b	0·37^b	1·48	0·62	a
Meath	0·14^b	0·19	—	a	0·13^b	0·49	a
Offaly	0·14^b	a	a	a	0·19^b	0·41	—
Westmeath	a	a	a	—	—	0·32	a
Wexford	4·07	0·48	a	—	0·07^b	0·95	—
Wicklow	0·47	2·45	1·40	0·60	0·60	0·51	a
Munster	0·66	0·28	1·83	0·67	0·65	1·10	0·34
Clare	a	0·24	a	—	—	0·62	a
Cork Co. Bor.	1·33	0·24	2·75	a	3·53	1·42	a
Cork Co.	0·68	0·09	4·98	a	0·87	1·26	0·17^b
Total Cork	0·83	0·13	4·41	a	1·49	1·29	0·16^b
Kerry	1·75	a	0·21^b	—	0·06^b	0·50	a
Limerick Co. Bor.	0·61	1·04	—	11·98	0·28	1·92	a
Limerick Co.	a	a	—	a	0·12^b	0·49	a
Total Limerick	0·26	0·42	—	4·44	0·18	1·02	a
Tipperary N.R.	a	—	a	—	a	1·84	a
Tipperary S.R.	0·17^b	—	a	—	0·14^b	0·72	2·30
Total Tipperary	0·13	—	a	—	0·09	1·22	1·38
Waterford Co. Bor.	0·88	3·95	a	—	a	3·31	—
Waterford Co.	a	0·21^a	a	—	a	0·51	a
Total Waterford	0·42	1·67	a	—	a	1·59	a
Connacht	0·09	0·33	0·21	a	0·10	0·45	0·30
Galway	0·14	a	0·49	a	0·13	0·41	0·55
Leitrim	a	a	—	a	a	0·27	a
Mayo	a	a	a	—	0·11	0·25	a
Roscommon	a	a	a	a	a	0·27	a
Sligo	0·18^b	0·04^b	a	—	a	1·35	a
Ulster (part of)	0·22	—	0·21	a	0·17	0·51	a
Cavan	0·28	0·07^b	a	—	—	0·87	a
Donegal	0·10^b	—	0·36^b	a	0·07^a	0·37	—
Monaghan	0·40	—	a	—	0·52^a	0·39	a

(a) Denotes less than 10 persons employed in the industry in the county.
(b) Denotes between 10 and 20 persons employed in the industry in the county.

	Fellmongery & leather dressing	Other leather & fur	Mining & quarrying	Turf production	Building & construction
Leinster	0·61	1·66	1·30	1·66	1·09
Carlow	3·83	a	2·08	—	0·92
Dublin Co. Bor.	0·39	2·58	0·15	0·12	1·16
Dunlaoire	—	0·65^b	0·20^b	0·17^b	1·42
Dublin Co.	0·18^b	1·01	0·53	0·20	1·38
Total Dublin	a	2·19	0·22	0·14	1·21
Kildare	a	a	1·48	10·23	0·95
Kilkenny	0·81^a	0·52^b	6·57	0·19	0·88
Laois	a	5·42	3·74	2·91	0·88
Longford	a	a	0·44^b	5·26	0·98
Louth	a	a	0·59	a	0·97
Meath	0·37^b	0·39^b	1·31	0·96	1·12
Offaly	a	1·24	0·16^b	17·17	0·90
Westmeath	0·93	a	0·22^b	4·35	1·06
Wexford	3·73	0·61	0·35	—	0·75
Wicklow	a	2·43	7·01	a	1·18
Munster	2·24	0·56	1·20	0·30	1·02
Clare	a	0·45^b	0·22	a	1·05
Cork Co. Bor.	0·33^b	1·18	0·64	—	1·28
Cork Co.	0·20	0·44	1·32	0·02^b	1·06
Total Cork	0·23	0·62	1·16	0·02^b	1·11
Kerry	0·70	0·62	0·40	0·49	0·88
Limerick Co. Bor.	2·58	a	a	—	1·20
Limerick Co.	a	0·86	0·29	a	0·99
Total Limerick	1·01	0·65	1·85	a	0·62
Tipperary N.R.	a	a	0·45	2·11	0·85
Tipperary S.R.	9·22	0·60^b	3·11	1·04	0·87
Total Tipperary	5·21	0·48	1·92	1·52	0·86
Waterford Co. Bor.	0·80^a	—	a	—	1·09
Waterford Co.	21·44	a	0·24^b	—	0·97
Total Waterford	13·43	a	0·15^b	—	1·02
Connacht	0·07^a	1·75	1·13	0·66	0·75
Galway	a	0·16^b	0·54	0·63	0·89
Leitrim	a	a	2·38	a	0·64
Mayo	a	a	0·14	0·91	0·58
Roscommon	a	a	2·92	1·11	0·77
Sligo	a	a	2·19	—	0·78
Ulster (part of)	0·51	0·28	0·69	0·27	0·80
Cavan	a	0·42^b	0·88	a	0·71
Donegal	a	a	0·34	0·50	0·88
Monaghan	2·14	0·46^b	1·19	—	0·74

(*a*) Denotes less than 10 persons employed in the industry in the county.
(*b*) Denotes between 10 and 20 persons employed in the industry in the county.

	Electricity	Gas	Transport & communication	Commerce	Insurance, banking & finance
Leinster	1·25	1·61	1·30	1·17	1·42
Carlow	0·45	—	0·51	1·09	0·63
Dublin Co. Bor.	1·48	2·90	1·93	1·39	1·97
Dunlaoire	1·43	3·21	1·59	1·51	3·40
Dublin Co.	1·46	1·24	1·15	1·22	2·20
Total Dublin	1·47	2·64	1·78	1·37	2·10
Kildare	1·35	—	0·63	0·85	0·47
Kilkenny	0·33	0·30[b]	0·55	0·83	0·63
Laois	2·11	—	0·60	0·81	0·45
Longford	0·59	—	0·45	0·76	0·47
Louth	1·25	1·04	1·21	1·15	0·72
Meath	0·38	—	0·53	0·80	0·45
Offaly	2·16	—	0·43	0·83	0·47
Westmeath	1·16	—	0·88	0·89	0·57
Wexford	0·39	0·57	0·81	1·00	0·59
Wicklow	0·69	0·93	1·00	1·04	0·90
Munster	0·90	0·74	0·89	0·96	0·77
Clare	0·93	—	0·61	0·59	0·42
Cork Co. Bor.	1·56	3·00	1·88	1·56	1·11
Cork Co.	0·76	0·73	0·76	0·92	0·96
Total Cork	0·95	1·26	1·02	1·07	0·99
Kerry	0·90	a	0·64	0·79	0·48
Limerick Co. Bor.	2·16	1·57	1·98	1·74	1·33
Limerick Co.	0·52	—	0·57	0·73	0·47
Total Limerick	1·12	0·60	1·09	1·10	0·79
Tipperary N.R.	0·47	—	0·63	0·82	0·58
Tipperary S.R.	0·41	0·56	0·61	0·92	0·63
Total Tipperary	0·44	0·40	0·61	0·87	0·61
Waterford Co. Bor.	1·89	2·32	2·08	1·48	1·04
Waterford Co.	0·51	—	0·50	0·81	0·61
Total Waterford	1·04	1·02	1·11	1·06	0·77
Connacht	0·58	0·10	0·51	0·66	0·43
Galway	0·49	0·12[b]	0·53	0·65	0·45
Leitrim	0·82	—	0·38	0·58	0·41
Mayo	0·45	a	0·50	0·65	0·36
Roscommon	0·53	a	0·41	0·59	0·38
Sligo	0·98	0·29[b]	0·69	0·83	0·63
Ulster (part of)	0·70	0·06[b]	0·51	0·79	0·42
Cavan	0·55	—	0·37	0·77	0·45
Donegal	0·89	—	0·64	0·77	0·37
Monaghan	0·47	0·24[b]	0·39	0·85	0·49

(a) Denotes less than 10 persons employed in the industry in the county.
(b) Denotes between 10 and 20 persons employed in the industry in the county.

	Professions	Public administration	Personal service	Entertainment & sport
Leinster	1·12	1·36	1·18	1·58
Carlow	0·91	0·50	1·02	0·52
Dublin Co. Bor.	1·22	1·84	1·26	2·29
Dunlaoire	1·93	1·36	2·19	2·50
Dublin Co.	1·52	1·56	1·32	1·87
Total Dublin	1·31	1·76	1·35	2·23
Kildare	0·78	2·40	1·08	2·30
Kilkenny	0·96	0·70	0·86	0·46
Laois	0·77	0·58	0·68	0·28
Longford	0·80	0·53	0·70	0·30
Louth	1·01	0·58	0·91	0·67
Meath	0·78	0·57	1·00	0·70
Offaly	0·74	0·44	0·58	0·25
Westmeath	1·07	1·75	0·88	0·66
Wexford	0·89	0·53	1·21	0·47
Wicklow	0·93	0·73	1·69	1·42
Munster	0·96	0·79	0·95	0·62
Clare	0·78	0·82	0·67	0·23
Cork Co. Bor.	1·14	1·40	1·13	1·13
Cork Co.	0·96	0·69	0·90	0·44
Total Cork	1·00	0·86	0·97	0·60
Kerry	0·81	0·61	0·94	0·34
Limerick Co. Bor.	1·32	1·67	1·38	1·47
Limerick Co.	0·87	0·48	0·90	0·33
Total Limerick	1·04	0·92	1·09	0·75
Tipperary N.R.	0·78	0·55	0·77	0·61
Tipperary S.R.	0·94	0·81	0·93	1·03
Total Tipperary	0·87	0·70	0·87	0·84
Waterford Co. Bor.	1·36	0·78	1·17	1·42
Waterford Co.	1·10	0·56	1·11	0·55
Total Waterford	1·20	0·64	1·15	0·89
Connacht	0·83	0·50	0·57	0·31
Galway	1·00	0·60	0·71	0·34
Leitrim	0·60	0·45	0·41	0·36
Mayo	0·71	0·41	0·50	0·27
Roscommon	0·74	0·46	0·40	0·20
Sligo	0·89	0·53	0·67	0·39
Ulster (part of)	0·76	0·58	0·77	0·30
Cavan	0·69	0·53	0·60	0·17
Donegal	0·72	0·58	0·91	0·31
Monaghan	0·93	0·62	0·66	0·42

BIBLIOGRAPHY

(1) P.S. Florence, *Investment, Location and Size of Plant*, Cambridge 1948.

(2) D. O'Mahony, *The Irish Economy*, Cork 1962.

(3) P. O'Malley, *The Structure and Performance of Irish Industry 1953-63*, M. Econ. Sc. degree thesis submitted to the National University of Ireland at University College, Dublin, September 1967.

(4) P.S. Florence, *The Logic of British and American Industry*, London 1953.

(5) *Report of the Survey Team established by the Minister for Agriculture on the Provender Milling Industry*, Dublin 1965.

(6) *Report of the Survey Team established by the Minister for Agriculture on the Dairy Products Industry*, Dublin 1963.

(7) W. Isward, 'Transport developments and business cycles' in *Quarterly Journal of Economics*, 57 (1942) 90–112.

(8) *Report of the Survey Team established by the Minister for Agriculture on the Beef, Mutton and Lamb Industry*, Dublin 1963.

(9) G.H. Hildebrand and A. J. Mace, 'The employment multiplier in an expanding industrial market: Los Angeles county 1940–47, in *The Review of Economics and Statistics*, 32 (1950) 241–249.

(10) R. Vining, 'Location of industry and regional patterns of business cycle behaviour' in *Econometrica*, 14 (1946) 37–68.

(11) C.M. Daly, 'An approximation to a geographical multiplier' in *The Economic Journal*, 50 (1940) 248–258.

(12) T. Baker, *Economic Research Institute Paper 32*, Dublin 1966.

(13) E.M. Hoover, *The Location of Economic Activity*, London 1958.

(14) Committee on Industrial Organisation, *A Synthesis of Reports by Survey Teams on Twenty-two Industries*, Dublin 1965.

(15) C.I.O., *Report on the Mantles and Gowns Industry*, Dublin 1963.

(16) C.I.O., *Report on the Men's and Boys' Outerwear Clothing Industry*, Dublin 1964.

(17) C.I.O., *Report on the Chemical Industry*, Dublin 1963.

(18) C.I.O., *Report on the Furniture Industry*, Dublin 1965.

(19) C.I.O., *Report on the Paper Products Industry*, Dublin 1964.

(20) C.I.O., *Report on the Printing Industry*, Dublin 1964.

(21) C.I.O., *Report on Processing of Fruit and Vegetables etc Industry*, Dublin 1964.

(22) G. Stigler, 'The division of labour is limited by the size of the market' in *Journal of Political Economy*, 59 (1951) 185–193.

(23) A.O. Hirchman, *The Strategy of Economic Development*, New Haven 1958.

(24) T. Scitovsky, 'Two concepts of external economies' in *Journal of Political Economy*, 62 (1954) 143–151.

(25) T.P. Linehan, 'The structure of Irish industry' in *Journal of the Statistical and Social Inquiry Society of Ireland*, 1961–62.

(26) M. Frankel, 'British and American manufacturing productivity' in *Bulletin No. 81*, University of Illinois, Urbana, 1957.

(27) P.S. Florence, *Postwar Investment, Location and Size of Plant*, Cambridge 1962.

(28) C.F. Carter and B.R. Williams, *Industry and Technical Progress*, London 1957.

(29) R. Eveley and I.M.D. Little, *Concentration in British Industry*, Cambridge 1960.

(30) I.H. Siegel, 'Aspects of productivity measurements and meaning' in *Productivity Measurements: Concepts*, 43–59, O.E.E.C. (E.P.A.) 1955.

(31) W.B. Reddaway and A. Smith, 'Progress in British manufacturing industry' in *The Economic Journal*, 70 (1960) 17–37.

(32) R.C. Geary, 'The concept of net volume of output' in *Journal of the Royal Statistical Society*, Parts III and IV (1944) 251–261.

(33) W.E. Salter, *Productivity and Technical Change*, Cambridge 1960.

(34) S. Fabricant, *Employment in Manufacturing*, N.B.E.R. 1940.

(35) E. Nevin, *Economic Research Institute Paper 12*, Dublin 1963.

(36) J.W. Kendrick, *Productivity Trends in the United States*, N.B.E.R. 1961.

(37) E.F. Dennison, 'Theoretical aspects of quality changes: capital consumption and net capital formation' in *Studies in Income and Wealth XIX*, N.B.E.R. 1957.

(38) E.E. Hagen, *On the Theory of Social Change*, Illinois 1962.

(39) E.D. Domar, 'On the measurement of technical change' in *The Economic Journal*, 71 (December 1961) 709–729.

(40) M. Abramovitz, 'Resource and output trends in the United States since 1870': *N.B.E.R. Occasional Paper 52*, New York 1956.

(41) R. Marris, *The Economics of Capital Utilisation*, Cambridge 1964.

(42) A.P. Usher, 'Industrialisation of modern Britain' in *Technology and Culture*, spring 1960.

(43) A.D. Kaplan, *Big Enterprise in a Competitive System,* Washington 1954.

(44) J.M. Clark, *Competition as a Dynamic Process,* Washington 1961.

(45) E. Penrose, *The Theory of the Growth of the Firm,* Oxford 1959.

(46) J.H. Dunning and C.J. Thomas, *British Industry,* London 1963.

(47) G.C. Allen, *The Structure of Industry in Britain,* London 1966.

(48) *Some Factors in Economic Growth in Europe During the 1950's,* United Nations 1964.

(49) *Science and Irish Economic Development I and II:* report of Research and Technology Survey Team appointed by the Minister for Industry and Commerce, Dublin 1966.

(50) R.J. Nicholson and S. Gupta, 'Output and productivity changes in British manufacturing industry 1948–54' in *Journal of the Royal Statistical Society,* series A, part 4 (1960) 427–459.

(51) K.S. Lomas, 'Growth and productivity movements in the U.K.' in *Productivity Measurement Review,* August 1964, 5–22.

(52) B.F. Massell, 'Capital formation and technological change in U.S. manufacturing', in *The Review of Economics and Statistics,* 42 (May 1960) 182–188.

(53) C.E.V. Leser, 'Commodity group expenditure functions for the U.K. 1948–57' in *Econometrica,* 29 (1961) 24–32.

(54) C.E.V. Leser, *Economic Research Institute Paper 4,* Dublin 1962.

(55) James McGilvray, *Irish Economic Statistics,* Dublin 1968.

(56) Kieran Kennedy, 'Growth of labour productivity in Irish manufacturing 1953–67' in *Journal of the Statistical and Social Inquiry Society of Ireland,* 1968–69.

(57) J. Cornwall, 'The role of investment demand in long-run growth' in *Quarterly Journal of Economics,* February 1970.

(58) J.A. Schumpeter, *The Theory of Economic Development,* Cambridge (Mass.) 1949.

SOURCES FOR TABLES

Table 1.1 *Census of Population 1961*, Volume 4, Table 5, 18–71.

Table 1.2 *O'Malley* (3), Chapter I, Table VII, which was derived from *Statistical Abstract 1963* (1961 data), Table 53, 70; Table 56, 78; Table 57, 80.
Census of Population 1961, Volume 4, Table 5, 18–71.

Table 1.3 Columns 1 and 2 derived from Attwood and Geary 'Irish county incomes in 1960' *Economic Research Institute Paper 16*, Dublin 1963, Table 2, 11.
Column 3 derived from column 1.
Columns 4, 5 and 6 from *Census of Population 1961*, Volume 4, Table 5, 18–71.

Table 1.4 *Census of Population 1961*, Volume 4, Table 5, 18–71.

Table 2.1 Florence classification schema derived from P.S. Florence, *Investment, Location and Size of Plant* (1). Table IIC, 17.

Table 2.2 *O'Malley* (3) Appendix B + C, Chapter II.

Table 2.3 *Statistical Abstract 1960* (1958 data), Table 109, 120; *O'Malley* (3), Appendix C, Chapter II. This appendix was derived as follows: column 1 from *Statistical Abstract 1960* (1958 data), Table 109, 120 and from the 1958 Census of Industrial Production published in *Irish Statistical Bulletin* December 1959, March, June, September 1960; columns 2 and 3 from *O'Malley* (3), Appendix B, Chapter II which was derived from the Supplement on the 1958 Census of Industrial Production published in *Irish Statistical Bulletin*, September 1960. Columns 4, 5 and 6 derived from P.S. Florence, *Postwar Investment, Location and Size of Plant* (27), Appendix A, 32–37.

Table 2.4 Columns 1, 2, and 5 from P.S. Florence, *Postwar Investment, Location and Size of Plant* (27), Appendix A, 32–37.
Column 3 from the Supplement on the 1958 Census of Industrial Production, *Irish Statistical Bulletin* September

139

1960. Column 4 from *Statistical Abstract 1960* (1958 data), Table 109, 120.

Table 3.1   Table 1.1 and *O'Malley* (3), Appendix C, Chapter II.

Table 3.2   As above.

Table 3.3   Table 1.1 and *Statistical Abstract 1961* (1958 data), Table 109, 122.

Table 3.4   Table 1.1 and 1958 Census of Industrial Production published in *Irish Statistical Bulletin,* December 1959, March, June and September 1960.

Table 4.1   *Statistical Abstract 1967* (1964 data), Table 106, 119 and *O'Malley* (3), Appendix A, Chapter V which was derived from information supplied by the Central Statistics Office.

Table 4.2   As above.

Table 4.3   As above.

Table 4.4   *O'Malley* (3), Appendix A, Chapter V which was derived from information supplied by the Central Statistics Office.

Table 4.5   As for Table 4.1

Table 4.6   As above.

Table 4.7   As above.

Table 4.8   Table 4.1.

Table 4.9   *O'Malley* (3), Appendix C, Chapter II and Appendix A, Chapter V.

Table 4.10   As above.

Table 4.11   *O'Malley* (3), Appendix A, Chapter V (columns 4 and 5).

Table 4.12   Table 1.1 and *O'Malley* (3), Appendix A, Chapter V.

Table 4.13   Industry horsepower data supplied by the Central Statistics Office (cf. *O'Malley* (3) Chapter IV, 12–17).

Table 4.14   As above.

Table 5.1   *O'Malley* (3), Chapter VII, Appendix A. which was derived as follows: column 1 taken from *Statictical Abstract 1966,* Table 111, 126. Other columns derived from column 1 and *Statistical Abstract 1956* (1953 data), Table 95, 109, *Statistical Abstract 1966,* Table 106, 119, and Census of Industrial Production for 1953 and 1963 published in *Irish Statistical Bulletin* September 1956, and September 1965.

Table 5.2   As above.

Table 5.3   As above.

Table 5.4   *Statistical Abstract 1966* (1963 data), Table 106, 119.

Table 6.1   *O'Malley* (3), Chapter VII, Appendix A and *Statistical Abstract 1956* (1953 data), Table 95, 109 and *Statistical Abstract 1966* (1963 data), Table 106, 119.

Table 6.2   *O'Malley* (3) Chapter VII, Appendix A.

Table 6.3   As above.

Table 6.4   Column 1 taken from *Science and Irish Economic Development* (49). Columns 2 and 3 derived from Tables 6.2 and 6.3.

Table 6.5   *United Nations Economic Survey*, 1961.

Table 7.1   Table 1.1 and as for Table 5.1.

Table 7.2   *O'Malley* (3), Appendix C, Chapter II, and as for Table 5.1.

Table 7.3   As for Table 4.13. and Table 5.1.

Table 7.4   *O'Malley* (3), Appendix A, Chapter V, and as for Table 5.1.

Table 7.5   Table 4.6 and as for Table 5.1.